To Paxton — I love you so much! I hope this book helps you know how much God loves you! May these conversations be life-giving to you! Love,
mama

IN THE EVENING

WHEN I REST

Life-Giving Conversations
with God

KATHERINE J. BUTLER

AMY MASON

RONALD A. BEERS

Tyndale House Publishers, Inc.
Carol Stream, Illinois

LIVING EXPRESSIONS COLLECTION

Living Expressions invites you to explore God's Word and express your creativity in ways that are refreshing to the spirit and restorative to the soul.

Visit Tyndale online at www.tyndale.com.

TYNDALE, Tyndale's quill logo, *Living Expressions*, and the Living Expressions logo are registered trademarks of Tyndale House Publishers, Inc.

In the Evening When I Rest: Life-Giving Conversations with God

Copyright © 2019 by Ronald A. Beers. All rights reserved.

Cover photo of stars copyright © by Casey Horner on Unsplash.com. All rights reserved.

Designed by Ron C. Kaufmann

Scripture quotations are adapted from the *Holy Bible*, New Living Translation, copyright © 1996, 2004, 2015 by Tyndale House Foundation. Used by permission of Tyndale House Publishers, Inc., Carol Stream, Illinois 60188. All rights reserved.

For information about special discounts for bulk purchases, please contact Tyndale House Publishers at csresponse@tyndale.com, or call 1-800-323-9400.

ISBN 978-1-4964-1810-4

Printed in China

25   24   23   22   21   20   19
7   6   5   4   3   2   1

INTRODUCTION

THINK BACK ON HOW YOU met your best friend. What bonded the two of you together? Certainly you enjoyed a lot of things in common; but more importantly, you *talked* to each other. You *listened* to each other. Without talking and listening, it is impossible to become close friends. Conversations are how we get to know a person—someone we can lean on in times of adversity; someone to share our joys and struggles; someone who will give us good advice; someone who will tell us the truth when we need to hear it. Moreover, through conversation we develop a level of trust that allows us to *rest* in that relationship—it becomes a safe haven.

Wouldn't you like to have a close friendship like that with God? If you are willing to invest the time needed to talk with him and listen to him, this book will help you begin to make that desire a reality. In fact, starting this very evening, you can enter into the rest that God promises.[1] It is possible to have a deep and trusting relationship with almighty God, just as you would any close friend. Indeed, God can be your closest friend—and he's available for conversation every morning, every evening, and every hour in between.

Do you long to hear God's voice more clearly? Do you wish he would speak into a situation you are currently facing? It can be tempting to believe that God is silent about the struggles and challenges you deal with every day. However, nothing could be further from the truth. He wants you to tell him what's on your mind, and he wants to tell you what is on *his* mind. God speaks to us primarily through his Word, the Bible. To hear him, you simply need to take the time to quiet yourself and listen—to read his Word and hear him speak through it. This book offers a unique way to help you do that.

In the Evening When I Rest poses many of the questions you may want to ask God. Over the course of one hundred evenings, you are certain to find many that you would love to hear God answer. What's wonderful is how God answers each of these questions in his Word.

Each reading begins with two related questions. The answers are drawn directly from the Bible, often using several verses woven together from different parts of Scripture. In some cases, the verses have been slightly paraphrased in voice or tense to keep with the theme of God talking directly to *you*.

God's Word is different and more powerful than any other book ever written. Because the Bible is a living document, conceived and inspired by God himself, it uniquely applies to each person who reads it, and God speaks uniquely to each individual through it—though of course there are also many truths and principles that apply to all people.

After you have spent time listening to God speak, pray the prayer that follows in each daily reading. These prayers are also taken directly from Scripture, and the wording has occasionally been adapted to fit the theme of your response to God. Let these prayers bless, inspire, and motivate you at the end of your day.

Following each reading, a short devotional thought or exercise will help you apply more deeply what you have read. This is the only part of the day's reading that is not adapted from God's Word.

Here are a few tips to help you get the most out of this devotional:

1. Read *slowly*. God's Word was never meant to be skimmed over. It is deep, rich, and worthy of your time. Let God's words sink into your heart, as if you were reading them for the first time.

2. Read *often*. We encourage you to stay committed to reading God's Word daily, because the more you read it, the more you will learn to recognize God's voice. Learning how to distinguish God's voice from your own, or from the voice of the enemy, has great power in your life.

3. Read *prayerfully*. Each evening, take a moment to settle into a quiet place, relax, and pray for an open heart as you learn from God's Word. Ask God to help you set aside distractions so you can be fully present and ready to receive his truth.

God has something to say to you about whatever issues and concerns you are facing. We pray that God will richly bless you as you ask him your questions, read his Word, and learn to recognize his voice. As the psalmist says, "It is good to proclaim your unfailing love in the morning, your faithfulness in the evening."[2] So, let your soul be at rest again, for the Lord has been good to you.[3]

GOD'S WORK OF TRANSFORMATION HAS ALREADY BEGUN

Lord, what happens when I begin to follow you?
Because of the Cross, your interest in this world has been crucified, and the world's interest in you has also died. What counts is whether you have been transformed into a new creation. Anyone who belongs to me has become a new person. The old life is gone. A new life has begun!

GALATIANS 6:14-15; 2 CORINTHIANS 5:17

If I'm a new person, why don't I feel different?
Can my life really change?
Don't copy the behavior and customs of this world, but let me transform you into a new person by changing the way you think. Do not despise these small beginnings, for I rejoice to see the work begin. You can be certain that I, who began the good work within you, will continue my work until it is finally finished on the day when I return.

ROMANS 12:2; ZECHARIAH 4:10; PHILIPPIANS 1:6

What can I pray as I'm preparing for a new beginning?
Help me abandon my shameful ways; for your regula-
tions are good. I long to obey your commandments!
Renew my life with your goodness.

PSALM 119:39-40

God has begun not only the work of salvation in your heart but also
the work of transforming your life. Where would you like to see the
greatest change this year? In a relationship? With an unhealthy
pattern or habit? Write a prayer of invitation, welcoming the Lord
to begin his transformative work in this area of your life.

DO YOU LONG FOR A FRESH START?

Lord, is it ever too late to start over with you?
I've washed away your sins and given you a new birth and new life through the Holy Spirit. Though your sins are like scarlet, I will make them as white as snow. Oh, return to me, for I have paid the price to set you free.

TITUS 3:5; ISAIAH 1:18; ISAIAH 44:22

Jesus, what story from Scripture shows your grace for those who need a fresh start?
As I was speaking, the teachers of religious law and the Pharisees brought a woman who had been caught in the act of adultery. "Teacher, this woman was caught in the act of adultery. The law of Moses says to stone her. What do you say?" They kept demanding an answer, so I stood up again and said, "All right, but let the one who has never sinned throw the first stone!" When the accusers heard this, they slipped away . . . until only I was left in the middle of the

crowd with the woman. I said to the woman, "Where are your accusers? Didn't even one of them condemn you?" "No, Lord," she said. And I said, "Neither do I. Go and sin no more." JOHN 8:3-11

What can I pray to remind myself of God's grace as I start over?
You have swept away my sins like a cloud. You have scattered my offenses like the morning mist.

ISAIAH 44:22

God delights in fresh starts and new beginnings. The same grace that Jesus showed the woman caught in adultery is the grace he extends to you. No sin is too big for God to forgive and redeem. Pray Isaiah 44:22 again, asking God for his grace to make a fresh start.

IT'S NEVER TOO LATE TO RETURN TO GOD

Lord, I've neglected our relationship for a long time. How do I begin again?

Come back to me and live! Only in returning to me and resting in me will you be saved. For the mountains may move and the hills disappear, but even then my faithful love for you will remain.

AMOS 5:4; ISAIAH 30:15; ISAIAH 54:10

Why would you allow me to neglect our relationship for so long?

I am being patient for your sake. I do not want anyone to be destroyed, but want everyone to repent. I must wait for you to come to me so I can show you my love and compassion. For I am a faithful God. Come close to me, and I will come close to you.   2 PETER 3:9; ISAIAH 30:18; JAMES 4:8

What can I pray to ask you to restore our relationship after a season of neglect?

O Lord, you are so good, so ready to forgive, so full of unfailing love for all who ask for your help. Teach me your ways, O LORD, that I may live according to your truth! Grant me purity of heart, so that I may honor you.   PSALM 86:5, 11

Distance in a relationship doesn't happen overnight but through many small decisions to give your attention to something else. However, even if you have neglected your relationship with God for a long time, it's never too late to start over. He promises to respond with grace and forgiveness. Move a small step closer toward God this evening. What can you choose to let go of to make time with God your priority? (Unnecessary errands? A TV show? Time on social media?)

HOW TO BUILD HEALTHY HABITS

Lord, why is it so hard to stick to healthy habits?
Don't you realize that you become the slave of whatever you choose to obey? For the spirit is willing, but the body is weak. Clothe yourself with my presence, and don't let yourself think about ways to indulge your evil desires. Don't copy the behavior and customs of this world, but let me transform you into a new person by changing the way you think.

ROMANS 6:16; MARK 14:38; ROMANS 13:14; ROMANS 12:2

How can you help me gain more self-control?
The Holy Spirit produces this kind of fruit in your life: love, joy, peace, patience, kindness, goodness, faithfulness, gentleness, and self-control. Make every effort to respond to my promises. Supplement knowledge with self-control, and self-control with patient endurance, and patient endurance with godliness.

GALATIANS 5:22-23; 2 PETER 1:5-6

What can I pray while I'm building new habits?
Guide my steps by your word, so I will not be overcome by evil. Give me a helping hand, for I have chosen to follow your commandments.

PSALM 119:133, 173

It's hard to change a habit unless you replace it with a new, healthier habit. Transformation is the process of God's renewal, replacing our habits of sin with habits of godliness. Where do you struggle the most with self-control right now? What bad habits are holding you back? Bring these needs to God in prayer and ask him for insight into how to replace old bad habits with new good habits.

SEEK AFTER THESE GOALS

*Lord, what principles should guide the goals
I set for myself?*

Are you seeking great things for yourself? Don't do it!
Seek the kingdom of God above all else, and live righteously. Love me with all your heart, all your soul, all
your mind, and all your strength. Love your neighbor
as yourself. Let love be your highest goal!

JEREMIAH 45:5; MATTHEW 6:33; MARK 12:30-31;
I CORINTHIANS 14:1

*Jesus, what actions will help me pursue love
and your Kingdom values?*

If you love only those who love you, why should you
get credit for that? Even sinners love those who love
them! You know what real love is because I gave up my
life for you. So you also ought to give up your life for
your brothers and sisters. Don't merely say that you love
others; show the truth by your actions. Do not get tired
of doing what is good. At just the right time you will
reap a harvest of blessing if you don't give up.

LUKE 6:32; I JOHN 3:16, 18; GALATIANS 6:9

What can I pray to motivate greater love in my heart?
This is real love—not that I loved you, but that you
loved me and sent your Son as a sacrifice to take away
my sins. Since you loved me that much, I surely ought
to love others.　I JOHN 4:10-11

*As a follower of Jesus, your main goal is to love God and love
others. How does God's Word encourage you to love him and others
well? How can you take a step toward making love your highest
goal? (For example: put someone ahead of yourself, put God
ahead of your to-do list, pray for those who have hurt you.)*

THE BEST WAY TO FACE ADVERSITY

Lord, why do you allow so much adversity in my life?
When troubles of any kind come your way, consider it an opportunity for great joy. These trials will show that your faith is genuine. It is being tested as fire tests and purifies gold—though your faith is far more precious than mere gold.   JAMES 1:2; 1 PETER 1:7

How is it even possible to have joy in a season of adversity?
For your present troubles are small and won't last very long. Yet they produce for you a glory that vastly outweighs them and will last forever! So don't look at the troubles you can see now; rather, fix your gaze on things that cannot be seen. For the things we see now will soon be gone, but the things we cannot see will last forever. Wait patiently for me. Be brave and courageous. Yes, wait patiently for me. I am your refuge and strength, always ready to help in times of trouble.

2 CORINTHIANS 4:17-18; PSALM 27:14; PSALM 46:1

What can I pray during my season of adversity?
Lord, don't hold back your tender mercies from me.
Let your unfailing love and faithfulness always protect
me. For troubles surround me—too many to count!
But may all who search for you be filled with joy and
gladness in you. You are my helper and my savior.
O my God, do not delay.   PSALM 40:11-12, 16-17

*How do you tend to respond when adversity comes your way?
Do you become discouraged? Angry? Hopeless? Think of a
trial you are currently facing and reread the verses above. How
might God be encouraging you to face adversity differently?
With patience? Courage? Hope?*

SEE HOW MUCH
HE CARES FOR YOU

*Lord, sometimes I feel like nobody cares about me.
Why would you care?*

Look at the lilies of the field and how they grow.
They don't work or make their clothing, yet Solomon
in all his glory was not dressed as beautifully as they
are. And if I care so wonderfully for wildflowers that
are here today and thrown into the fire tomorrow,
I will certainly care for you. Why do you have so
little faith?   MATTHEW 6:28-30

*How can I have more faith that you will always
care for me?*

Give all your worries and cares to me, for I care about
you. Listen to me; I have cared for you since you were
born. Yes, I carried you before you were born. I will be
your God throughout your lifetime—until your hair
is white with age. I made you, and I will care for you.

I PETER 5:7; ISAIAH 46:3-4

What can I pray to remind myself to trust in your care?
What are mere mortals that you should think about
us, human beings that you should care for us? Yet you
made us only a little lower than you and crowned
us with glory and honor. I will be glad and rejoice in
your unfailing love, for you have seen my troubles,
and you care about the anguish of my soul.

PSALM 8:4-5; PSALM 31:7

*God's care for you is deeply personal. He created you to have
a relationship with him. Make a point to connect with God this
evening—even if it's in your pain. Write down your worries and
cares as a prayer, and remind yourself of the truth that God is
with you and has always been with you; that he is listening;
and that he cares about every item you wrote down.*

A GOOD LEADER KNOWS WHO TO FOLLOW

Jesus, what can I learn from you as a leader?
If any of you wants to be my follower, you must give up your own way, take up your cross daily, and follow me. If you try to hang on to your life, you will lose it. But if you give up your life for my sake, you will save it. LUKE 9:23-24

Jesus, what is the key to effective leadership?
Whoever wants to be a leader among you must be your servant, and whoever wants to be first among you must become your slave. For even I, the Son of Man, came not to be served but to serve others and to give my life as a ransom for many. I do nothing on my own but say only what the Father taught me. And the one who sent me is with me—he has not deserted me. For I always do what pleases him.

MATTHEW 20:26-28; JOHN 8:28-29

What should I pray for those I lead?

Who am I to lead the people? May integrity and honesty protect me, for I put my hope in you. Show me the right path, O LORD. I will pursue your commands, for you expand my understanding. God, may you be merciful and bless us. May your face smile with favor on us.

EXODUS 3:11; PSALM 25:21; PSALM 25:4;
PSALM 119:32; PSALM 67:1

Jesus surrendered his life to God his Father. He showed us that in the Kingdom of Heaven, the greatest leader is the one who serves others. Where do you have a leadership role? At work? At church? As a parent? What are the opportunities you have to follow Jesus' model as a servant leader? Some examples might be: helping your children pick up their toys; encouraging those you lead to volunteer at a soup kitchen or local shelter; offering to take a project no one else wants in order to help your boss or company.

GOD CAN BRING GOOD FROM ANY CIRCUMSTANCE

Lord, do you send both joyful and troubling circumstances my way?

I create the light and make the darkness. I send good times and bad times. I, the LORD, am the one who does these things. Enjoy prosperity while you can, but when hard times strike, realize that both come from me. ISAIAH 45:7; ECCLESIASTES 7:14

But why would you allow me to face such adversity?

Don't be surprised at the fiery trials you are going through, as if something strange were happening to you. Instead, be very glad—for these trials make you partners with Christ in his suffering, so that you will have the wonderful joy of seeing his glory when it is revealed to all the world. So if you are suffering in a manner that pleases me, keep on doing what is right, and trust your life to me, the God who created you, for I will never fail you. 1 PETER 4:12-13, 19

What can I pray during difficult times?

Great is your faithfulness; your mercies begin afresh each morning. I say to myself, "The LORD is my inheritance; therefore, I will hope in him!" For no one is abandoned by you forever. Though you bring grief, you also show compassion because of the greatness of your unfailing love.

LAMENTATIONS 3:23-24, 31-32

God uses both good and difficult circumstances to shape you into the person he wants you to be. Remember, your character and faith are important parts of who you are. Whether you are currently living in sunshine or storms, God loves you, he is with you, and he is able to bring good out of any situation. Can you remember a difficult circumstance in your life that God used for good? How can this encourage your faith in today's circumstances?

THERE CAN BE JOY
DESPITE YOUR TROUBLES

Lord, when trouble comes, what hope
will bring me joy?
Walk along the path of my commands, for that is
where your happiness is found. When you call on me,
I will answer; I will be with you in trouble.

PSALM 119:35; PSALM 91:15

How can I be happy about my troubles, Jesus?
What does that mean?
Because of the joy awaiting me, I endured the cross,
disregarding its shame. Now I am seated in the
place of honor beside my Father's throne. Because
of your faith, I have brought you into this place of
undeserved privilege where you now stand, and you
can confidently and joyfully look forward to sharing my glory. HEBREWS 12:2; ROMANS 5:2

What can I pray when I lose sight of the
eternal joy awaiting me?

Even though the fig trees have no blossoms, and there are no grapes on the vines; even though the olive crop fails, and the fields lie empty and barren; even though the flocks die in the fields, and the cattle barns are empty, yet I will rejoice in you, LORD! I will be joyful in you, the God of my salvation!

HABAKKUK 3:17-18

Happiness alone isn't the goal of our faith. Happiness is too elusive to be the basis of our trust in Jesus. Our faith is based on the eternal love of God and the work of Jesus on the cross. This is what allows us to experience joy despite our troubles. What problem are you facing right now? Frame your own prayer using the words of Habakkuk 3. Insert your own troubles and words into this prayer and focus on the desire to find joy in God as your hope and helper during this time. For example:
Even though _____, yet I will rejoice in you, Lord!

STAY ON GOD'S PATH TO AVOID GETTING LOST

Lord, how can I discern your will for my life?

Be still, and know that I am God! I will guide you along the best pathway for your life. I will advise you and watch over you. I am the LORD your God, who teaches you what is good for you and leads you along the paths you should follow. Come, my children, and listen to me.

PSALM 46:10; PSALM 32:8; ISAIAH 48:17; PSALM 34:11

How can I be sure I'm on the right path?

My paths are true and right, and righteous people live by walking in them. Tune your ears to wisdom, ask for understanding, and you will gain knowledge of me. My sheep listen to my voice; I know them, and they follow me. Your own ears will hear me. Right behind you a voice will say, "This is the way you should go," whether to the right or to the left.

HOSEA 14:9; PROVERBS 2:2-3, 5; JOHN 10:27; ISAIAH 30:21

*As I wake up each morning, how can I pray
to follow your path for the day?*

Show me the right path, O LORD; point out the road
for me to follow. Lead me by your truth and teach me,
for you are the God who saves me.   PSALM 25:4-5

Discerning God's will only happens when we are connected to him.
God promises to help us hear his voice and to guide us if we are committed to listening. Take time to invite him into your plans and
decisions—both big and small. Ask him the following questions as
you think about your day: Have I spent enough time being quiet, still,
and open to hearing your voice? Have I absorbed your Word today?
Is there anything in my day that hinders me from hearing you? How
can I better remind myself of your presence throughout the day?

DO NOT NEGLECT MEETING TOGETHER

Lord, how can I avoid feeling lonely and isolated?
There are "friends" who destroy each other, but a
real friend sticks closer than a brother. Christians
are all parts of Christ's body, and you all belong
to each other. Do not neglect meeting together,
as some people do, but encourage one another,
especially now that the day of my return is
drawing near.

PROVERBS 18:24; ROMANS 12:5;
HEBREWS 10:25

*How can I build close connections
and true friendships?*
When you get together, encourage your friends in
their faith, but also be encouraged by theirs. Don't
just pretend to love others. Really love them. Love
each other with genuine affection, and take delight
in honoring each other. When your friends are in
need, be ready to help them. Always be eager to

practice hospitality. Be happy with those who are happy, and weep with those who weep.

ROMANS 1:12; ROMANS 12:9-15

What can I pray when I feel alone?
Don't leave me now; don't abandon me, O God of my salvation! Even if my father and mother abandon me, you will hold me close.   PSALM 27:9-10

The world is more connected today than ever. With smartphones and social media, we are only a click away from our friends. Yet many people report feeling more isolated and lonely than ever. Think about your daily connections with others. Are they mostly through social media? How often do you see your friends in person, connecting face-to-face and encouraging one another? Schedule a time to meet with a friend this week. Have him or her over for dinner, or meet for lunch, with the intention of building a deeper sense of connection and community.

LOVE GOD. LOVE OTHERS. THAT'S ALL.

Lord, I long to find community. Do you desire this for me too?

My great desire is that you will keep on loving others as long as life lasts. For the whole law can be summed up in this one command: "Love your neighbor as yourself." Love each other with genuine affection, and take delight in honoring each other. Confess your sins to each other and pray for each other. Share each other's burdens, and in this way obey the law of Christ.

HEBREWS 6:11; GALATIANS 5:14;
ROMANS 12:10; JAMES 5:16; GALATIANS 6:2

Can I build strong friendships with nonbelievers?

Matthew invited me and my disciples to his home as dinner guests, along with many tax collectors and other disreputable sinners. When the Pharisees saw this, they asked my disciples, "Why does your teacher eat with such scum?" When I heard this, I said, "Healthy people don't need a doctor—sick people do. For I have come to call not those who think they are righteous, but those who know they are sinners." For I was reconciling the world to myself, no longer counting people's sins against them. This is the wonderful message I have given you to tell others.

MATTHEW 9:10-13; 2 CORINTHIANS 5:19

What can I pray as I search for community?
May you grant my heart's desires and make all my plans succeed.   PSALM 20:4

Searching for community can feel lonely, discouraging, and uncomfortable. Real community takes time and effort. But remember: Each interaction could be the beginning of a beautiful friendship. Pray tonight for God to place you in a godly, encouraging, gracious, authentic, life-giving, and loving community. Trust God to reward your efforts as you pursue fellowship.

WHO'S DRIVING YOUR LIFE?

Lord, I'm feeling lost right now. Can you get me back on track?

Come back to me and live! Listen to me, for all who follow my ways are joyful. I will guide you along the best pathway for your life. I will advise you and watch over you. Do what is right and good in my sight, so all will go well with you. I want to see a mighty flood of justice, an endless river of righteous living.

AMOS 5:4; PROVERBS 8:32; PSALM 32:8; DEUTERONOMY 6:18; AMOS 5:24

How can I live purposefully as I wait to see how you work in me?

I am the vine; you are the branches. Those who remain in me, and I in them, will produce much fruit. For apart from me you can do nothing. Be strong and immovable. Always work enthusiastically for me, for you know that nothing you do for me is ever useless.

JOHN 15:5; 1 CORINTHIANS 15:58

How can I pray for purposeful direction?

Have mercy on me, O God, have mercy! I look to you for protection. I will hide beneath the shadow of your wings until the danger passes by. I cry out to you, God Most High. You will fulfill your purpose for me.

PSALM 57:1-2

*W*hen you're in a season where God seems quiet, it's easy to feel as if your life has no direction. But these verses remind us that even when we feel lost, we are not lost to God. Find a moment to sit in your car—on the passenger side. Use this as a prayer moment to surrender to God and invite him to steer your life in the direction he wants it to go. Thank him for your ultimate eternal destination and that he can be trusted to pick out the best route between here and there.

YOUR LIFE IS MORE THAN THE SUM OF YOUR POSSESSIONS

Lord, how do I know if I have too much stuff?
Don't store up treasures here on earth; store your
treasures in heaven. Wherever your treasure is,
there the desires of your heart will also be. For you
died to this life, and your real life is hidden with
Christ, who richly gives you all you need for your
enjoyment.

MATTHEW 6:19–21; COLOSSIANS 3:3;
1 TIMOTHY 6:17

*How can I own things and yet not allow
my things to own me?*
No one can serve two masters. For you will hate
one and love the other; you will be devoted to one
and despise the other. You cannot serve me and be
enslaved to money. Some people, craving money,
have wandered from the true faith and pierced
themselves with many sorrows. Those who love

money will never have enough. How meaningless to think that wealth brings true happiness!

MATTHEW 6:24; I TIMOTHY 6:10; ECCLESIASTES 5:10

What can I pray to remind myself to keep you first? Your unfailing love is better than life itself; how I praise you! You satisfy me more than the richest feast. I will praise you with songs of joy. PSALM 63:3, 5

When you become overly focused on cleaning, caring for, and protecting your possessions, they end up owning you instead of the other way around. One of the best ways to fight against materialism is through generosity. Find a way to give generously this week. Donate to an organization, pay for someone's groceries at the store, or give a little more to your church than you are comfortable with. Your heart follows where you invest your money. Viewing your money and possessions as gifts from God you can use to bless others is the path to freedom from materialism.

UNCLUTTER YOUR LIFE

Lord, how can I live simply?

Don't worry about everyday life—whether you have enough food to eat or enough clothes to wear. Life is more than food, and your body more than clothing. Look at the ravens. They don't plant or harvest or store food in barns, for my Father feeds them. And you are far more valuable to him than any birds! This world is fading away, along with everything that people crave. But anyone who does what pleases me will live forever. LUKE 12:22-24; 1 JOHN 2:17

But is simplicity even possible in this complicated, busy world?

You are worried and upset over all these details! There is only one thing worth being concerned about: Love me with all your heart, all your soul, all your strength, and all your mind. And love your neighbor as yourself. Do this and you will live!

LUKE 10:41-42; LUKE 10:27-28

What can I pray to focus on simple living?

Father, may your name be kept holy. May your Kingdom come soon. Give me each day the food I need, and forgive my sins as I forgive those who sin against me. And don't let me yield to temptation.

LUKE 11:2-4

Simplicity is letting go of the things that clutter and complicate your life in order to better focus on the more fulfilling life that Jesus promises. It's not about getting rid of all your things but rather about experiencing freedom from being a slave to them. Which area in your life do you feel the Lord calling you to simplify? Your possessions? Expectations? Perfectionism? Schedule? Commitments? Ask God to help you learn how to let go in order to experience real freedom by focusing on what really matters.

ARE YOU TEACHABLE?

*Lord, what are the attributes of someone with
a teachable heart?*

Wise people treasure knowledge, but the babbling of a
fool invites disaster. Intelligent people are always ready
to learn. Their ears are open for knowledge. Fools think
their own way is right, but the wise listen to others.
Fools have no interest in understanding; they only want
to air their own opinions. A prudent person foresees
danger and takes precautions. The simpleton goes
blindly on and suffers the consequences.

PROVERBS 10:14; PROVERBS 18:15;
PROVERBS 12:15; PROVERBS 18:2; PROVERBS 22:3

How can I become more open to your instruction?

My child, listen to what I say, and treasure my commands. Tune your ears to wisdom, and concentrate on
understanding. Cry out for insight, and ask for understanding. Search for them as you would for silver; seek
them like hidden treasures. Then you will understand
what it means to fear me, and you will gain knowledge of who I am. Then you will understand what is

right, just, and fair, and you will find the right way
to go.   PROVERBS 2:1-5, 9

What can I pray to ready my heart to learn?
Teach me your ways, O LORD, that I may live according to your truth!   PSALM 86:11

*Think about the contrast between the wise person and the fool
in the verses above. Are you open to what the Lord wants to
teach you in every circumstance? In conversations with others,
do you tend to talk more than you listen? Ask someone, "What can
I do to be a better _____ (spouse, parent, boss, friend,
sibling, coworker, neighbor)?" Before you ask, reread the
Scriptures above to gain wisdom about how to approach this
conversation. Ask God for his insight and wisdom as you listen.*

RELEASE CONTROL AND RECEIVE SO MUCH MORE

Lord, how can I let go of trying to control everything?
If you cling to your life, you will lose it, and if you let your life go, you will save it. Humble yourself before me. Trust in me with all your heart; do not depend on your own understanding. Seek my will in all you do, and I will show you which path to take.

LUKE 17:33; JAMES 4:10; PROVERBS 3:5-6

How can I release control yet also plan for the future?
You can make your plans, but I determine your steps. Look here, you who say, "Today or tomorrow we are going to a certain town and will stay there a year. We will do business there and make a profit." How do you know what your life will be like tomorrow? Your life is like the morning fog—it's here a little while, then it's gone. What you ought to say is, "If the Lord wants us to, we will live and do this or that."

PROVERBS 16:9; JAMES 4:13-15

*What can I pray when I find myself trying
to control everything?*

My old self has been crucified with you, Jesus. It is no
longer I who live, but you who live in me. So I live
in this earthly body by trusting you, the Son of God,
who loved me and gave yourself for me.

GALATIANS 2:20

*Releasing control over your own plans opens your hands to grasp
God's plan. And God's plan is always for your ultimate good.
Is there something you need to release your grip on? Write down
your plans and prayerfully submit each one to God. Ask him
to help you trust that he knows what is best for you.*

HIS PLANS WILL UNFOLD AT THE RIGHT TIME

My timetable doesn't seem to be aligning with yours right now, Jesus. How can I trust your timing?
While I was teaching in the Temple, the leaders tried to arrest me; but no one laid a hand on me, because my time had not yet come. When you were utterly helpless, I came at just the right time and died for sinners. I gave my life to purchase freedom for everyone. For I know the plans I have for you. They are plans for good and not for disaster, to give you a future and a hope.

JOHN 7:30; ROMANS 5:6; I TIMOTHY 2:6;
JEREMIAH 29:11

What can I be doing as I wait for your timing?
Never be lazy, but work hard and serve me enthusiastically. Rejoice in your confident hope. Be patient in trouble, and keep on praying. Cry out to me, for I will fulfill my purpose for you.

ROMANS 12:11-12; PSALM 57:2

What can I pray as I watch for your plans to unfold?
I keep praying to you, LORD, hoping this time you
will show me favor. In your unfailing love, O God,
answer my prayer with your sure salvation.

PSALM 69:13

Are you waiting on something from the Lord right now? Ask him how he might want you to use this time of waiting. Does he want you to practice patience? Be hopeful? Pray? Find gratitude or contentment in this circumstance? Serve someone? As you wait for God to do his work in situations you can't control, don't be idle. Serve him where you are, as best as you know how.

LIVE INTENTIONALLY

Lord, how can I be more intentional with those I love?
Do to others as you would like them to do to you.
Don't look out only for your own interests, but
take an interest in others, too. Think of ways to
motivate others to acts of love and good works.
Encourage others. Live in harmony and peace.
Let everything you say be good and helpful, so
that your words will be an encouragement to
those who hear them.

LUKE 6:31; PHILIPPIANS 2:4; HEBREWS 10:24;
2 CORINTHIANS 13:11; EPHESIANS 4:29

*What does intentionality within a
community look like?*
All the believers devoted themselves to the apostles'
teaching, and to fellowship, and to sharing in meals,
and to prayer. They met together in one place and
shared everything they had. They shared with those
in need. They worshiped together each day, met in
homes for the Lord's Supper, and shared their meals

with great joy and generosity—all the while praising me and enjoying the goodwill of all the people.

ACTS 2:42, 44-47

How can I pray to be more intentional with others?
I pray that my love will overflow more and more, and that I will keep on growing in knowledge and understanding. PHILIPPIANS 1:9

It is easy to become so focused on our own issues that we forget to think about others. God calls us to be intentional with those he has placed in our circle of influence. Intentionality doesn't happen on its own—it takes effort. Who is someone God might be calling you to take more of an interest in? To make an effort to meet with regularly? To love and encourage in his or her faith? What is one intentional way you can reach out to that person today?

EVERY GOOD THING
COMES FROM GOD

Lord, what does it mean to depend on you?
I am your Master! Every good thing you have comes
from me. Do not think you are qualified to do anything on your own. Your qualification comes from
me. Trust in me at all times. Pour out your heart to
me, for I am your refuge.

PSALM 16:2; 2 CORINTHIANS 3:5; PSALM 62:8

What are the benefits of depending on you, Lord?
I am the vine; you are a branch. If you remain in me,
and I in you, you will produce much fruit. For apart
from me you can do nothing. But blessed are you if
you trust in me and make me your hope and confidence. You will be like a tree planted along a riverbank, with roots that reach deep into the water. Such
a tree is not bothered by the heat or worried by long
months of drought. Your leaves will stay green, and
you will never stop producing fruit.

JOHN 15:5; JEREMIAH 17:7-8

*Father, what can I pray to deepen
my dependence on you?*

O my God, I thank you and praise your glorious
name! But who am I, that I could give anything to
you? Everything I have has come from you, and I
give you only what you first gave me!

I CHRONICLES 29:13-14

*Depending on God means that your trust is deeply rooted in
him; thus, whatever you do, it is for his glory and by his grace.
Dependence on God isn't weakness but confidence that you
are connected to the one who is the giver of all good gifts. Make
a gratitude list this evening. Write down every blessing God
has given you. Review your list regularly, thanking the Lord
that you can place your hope and confidence in him.*

MIRACLES ARE ALL AROUND YOU

Lord, do you still perform miracles today?

I do great things too marvelous to understand. I perform countless miracles. For I am able, through my mighty power at work within you, to accomplish infinitely more than you might ask or think. With me, everything is possible.

JOB 9:10; EPHESIANS 3:20; MATTHEW 19:26

I need a miracle in my life. Can I ask you for one?

Keep on asking, and you will receive what you ask for. For everyone who asks, receives. Everyone who seeks, finds. And to everyone who knocks, the door will be opened. You parents—if your children ask for a loaf of bread, do you give them a stone instead? Of course not! So if you sinful people know how to give good gifts to your children, how much more will I give good gifts to those who ask me.

MATTHEW 7:7-11

*What can I pray when asking you for a
miracle in my life?*

O Sovereign LORD! You made the heavens and earth
by your strong hand and powerful arm. Nothing is
too hard for you! Listen to my voice in the morning,
LORD. Each morning I bring my requests to you and
wait expectantly. Because of my faith in Jesus, I can
now come boldly and confidently into your presence.
LORD, hear me and help me!

JEREMIAH 32:17; PSALM 5:3; EPHESIANS 3:12;
JEREMIAH 18:19

*Miracles happen every day—the birth of a baby, an awesome
sunset, the restoration of a hopeless relationship, the rebirth of
the earth in spring. If you think you've never seen a miracle,
ask God to open your eyes to the miracles all around you. What is
something you have wanted to ask of God but felt was too
impossible, even for him? Allow these verses to give you the courage
to pray for that right now, remembering that God is able to do
infinitely more than you could ever ask or imagine.*

COME AND LISTEN

Lord, what can I learn from listening to you?
Listen to me. I have cared for you since you were born. Come and listen to my counsel. I'll share my heart with you and make you wise. I will teach you to fear me. I will teach you wisdom's ways and lead you in straight paths. Let those who are wise understand these things. Let those with discernment listen carefully. My paths are true and right, and righteous people live by walking in them.

ISAIAH 46:3; PROVERBS 1:23; PSALM 34:11; PROVERBS 4:11; HOSEA 14:9

How can I listen to you better?
Be still, and know that I am God! Each morning bring your requests to me and wait expectantly. Pay attention to how you hear. To those who listen to my teaching, more understanding will be given. But for those who are not listening, even what they think they understand will be taken away from them.

PSALM 46:10; PSALM 5:3; LUKE 8:18

How can I pray to ready my heart to hear from you?
You are near, O LORD, and all your commands are true. I have known from my earliest days that your laws will last forever. My heart has heard you say, "Come and talk with me." And my heart responds, "LORD, I am coming." Let all that I am wait quietly before you, for my hope is in you.

PSALM 119:151-152; PSALM 27:8; PSALM 62:5

God has so much he wants to share with you! When was the last time you heard the Lord speak to you? Take a moment right now to pray, "Lord, what do you want to say to me about this day?" Wait quietly and reflect on what comes to mind. Ask yourself whether those thoughts line up with Scripture. Are they words of love and grace? Do they point you toward God and his Kingdom?

JUST BE YOURSELF

Lord, I'm tired of pretending to have it all together. How can I be authentic in my relationship with you?

Everyone has sinned; all fall short of my glorious standard. If you claim you have no sin, you are only fooling yourself and not living in the truth. But if you confess your sins to me, I am faithful and just to forgive your sins and cleanse you from all wickedness. Give all your worries and cares to me, for I care about you.

ROMANS 3:23; 1 JOHN 1:8-9; 1 PETER 5:7

How can I be more authentic with others?

Don't just pretend to love others. Really love them. Hate what is wrong. Hold tightly to what is good. And don't think you know it all! Confess your sins to each other and pray for each other so that you may be healed. ROMANS 12:9, 16; JAMES 5:16

*What can I pray to ask you to help me
live authentically?*

Help me abandon my shameful ways; for your regulations are good. I long to obey your commandments! Renew my life with your goodness. May integrity and honesty protect me, for I put my hope in you.

PSALM 119:39-40; PSALM 25:21

It is human nature to cover up the messes in our lives. Maybe you think that if you portray a picture-perfect image, others will see you as successful and self-sufficient. It is humbling to admit you have struggles, yet this is the first step in bringing authenticity to your life with God and others. Be vulnerable with God by allowing him into the messiness of your life. What are you anxious about? Where do you notice feelings of jealousy or envy? Whom do you want to impress, and to what lengths will you go to gain admiration? Read Romans 3:23-24 and experience God's love and forgiveness.

WHEN LIFE FEELS UNSATISFYING

Lord, why do I sometimes feel so empty inside?
Idols are all foolish, worthless things. All your idols
are as empty as the wind. Why spend your money
on food that does not give you strength? Why pay
for food that does you no good? Listen to me, and
you will eat what is good. You will enjoy the fin-
est food. I am the bread of life. Whoever comes to
me will never be hungry again. Whoever believes in
me will never be thirsty. Come to me with your ears
wide open. Listen, and you will find life.

ISAIAH 41:29; ISAIAH 55:2; JOHN 6:35;
ISAIAH 55:3

What is the secret to a truly fulfilling life?
In Christ lives all the fullness of me in a human body.
So you also are complete through your union with
him, who is the head over every ruler and authority.
My purpose is to give you a rich and satisfying life.

COLOSSIANS 2:9-10; JOHN 10:10

What can I pray when my life feels empty?
Let all that I am praise you, LORD; with my whole
heart, I will praise your holy name. Let all that I am
praise you, LORD; may I never forget the good things
you do for me. You fill my life with good things.
My youth is renewed like the eagle's!

PSALM 103:1-2, 5

*Jesus often used images of food and drink (the bread and the cup)
as analogies for our spiritual dependence on him. Just as our bodies
depend on nourishment from food to sustain us, so our souls depend
on the gracious work of Jesus Christ. Next time you celebrate
Communion, reflect on the truth that God is the nourishment
and satisfaction your heart most longs for.*

SLOW DOWN AND SAVOR

Why is it important to slow down sometimes?
Be still, and know that I am God. I have made your
life no longer than the width of your hand. Your entire
lifetime is just a moment to me, and all your busy
rushing ends in nothing. How do you know what your
life will be like tomorrow? Your life is like the morning
fog—it's here a little while, then it's gone. When Jesus
said, "Let's go off by ourselves to a quiet place and rest
awhile," he said this because there were so many people
coming and going that he and his apostles didn't even
have time to eat.

PSALM 46:10; PSALM 39:5-6; JAMES 4:14;
MARK 6:31

*Lord, what happens when I take time out of
my busy schedule to slow down?*
Be still in my presence, and wait patiently for me to
act. Come to me, all of you who are weary and carry
heavy burdens, and I will give you rest. Take my yoke
upon you. Let me teach you, because I am humble
and gentle at heart, and you will find rest for your

souls. Only in returning to me and resting in me will you be saved. In quietness and confidence is your strength.

PSALM 37:7; MATTHEW 11:28-29; ISAIAH 30:15

What can I pray when I find myself always rushing? Those who live in the shelter of the Most High will find rest in the shadow of the Almighty. This I declare about you, LORD: You alone are my refuge, my place of safety; you are my God, and I trust you.

PSALM 91:1-2

When you rush through life, it's easy to miss out on all that God has waiting for you today. Intentionally fight against hurry by slowly reading the Bible verses on this page once again. Savor each word. Was there anything you missed the first time you read through them?

DON'T SLIP BACK INTO YOUR OLD WAYS

Lord, what should I do if I've drifted away from you?
Everyone has sinned; everyone falls short of my glorious standard. Yet I, in my grace, freely make you right in my sight. I did this through Christ Jesus when he freed you from the penalty for your sins. Now this is what I say: "Come back to me and live!" Confess all your sins to me and stop trying to hide your guilt. Say to yourself, "I will confess my rebellion to the Lord." I forgive you! All your guilt is gone.

ROMANS 3:23-24; AMOS 5:4; PSALM 32:5

How can I stay close to you?
You must live as my obedient children. Don't slip back into your old ways of living to satisfy your own desires. You didn't know any better then. But now you must be holy in everything you do, just as I who chose you am holy. Keep watch and pray, so that you

will not give in to temptation. For the spirit is willing, but the body is weak!

1 PETER 1:14-15; MATTHEW 26:41

What can I pray when I long to reconnect with you?
Remember, O LORD, your compassion and unfailing love, which you have shown from long ages past. Do not remember the rebellious sins of my youth. Remember me in the light of your unfailing love, for you are merciful, O LORD.   PSALM 25:6-7

Sometimes patterns of behavior can be so deeply ingrained that we fall back into them without realizing it. At other times, we make an intentional decision. Either way, a healthy spiritual life means moving forward, growing to be more and more like Christ. If you've fallen back into old patterns of sin, pray the prayer above to ask for God's forgiveness. As you do, imagine God with open arms, calling to you, "Come back to me!"

DON'T BE ENSLAVED TO SHAME

*Lord, how can I experience freedom from
the shame of my past?*

Fear not; you will no longer live in shame. Don't be
afraid; there is no more disgrace for you. You will no
longer remember the shame of your youth. For I am
your Redeemer, the Holy One of Israel, the God of
all the earth. I have called you back from your grief—
as though you were a young wife abandoned by her
husband.   ISAIAH 54:4-6

But what if I still feel guilty, Lord?

There is no condemnation for those who belong to
me. And because you belong to me, the power of
my life-giving Spirit has freed you from the power
of sin that leads to death. Even if you feel guilty,
I am greater than your feelings.

ROMANS 8:1-2; I JOHN 3:20

What can I pray when I need to be lifted out of shame?
When I look to you for help, I will be radiant with joy;
no shadow of shame will darken my face. You surround
and defend all who fear you. You will redeem those
who serve you. No one who takes refuge in you will be
condemned.   PSALM 34:5, 7, 22

*Any thought or feeling that tries to convince you that you are
unlovable, unworthy, and beyond help is not from God. He says you
are loved, you are redeemed, and you belong to him. Are you worried that a mistake from your past or something that happened to
you will define you? Write down your fear and read the prayer
above again. Destroy or throw away the written expression of your
fear as a symbol of how God treats your past mistakes.*

GOD CAN WORK THROUGH YOU TO DO GREAT THINGS

Lord, how have you used unlikely people to do great things?

Moses pleaded with me, "O Lord, I'm not very good with words. I never have been, and I'm not now, even though you have spoken to me. I get tongue-tied, and my words get tangled." Then I asked Moses, "Who makes a person's mouth? Who decides whether people speak or do not speak, hear or do not hear, see or do not see? Is it not I, the LORD? Now go! I will be with you as you speak, and I will instruct you in what to say." EXODUS 4:10-12

How can you use me despite my limitations?

You didn't choose me. I chose you. I appointed you to go and produce lasting fruit. For I am working in you, giving you the desire and the power to do what pleases me. Don't be discouraged, for I am your God. I will strengthen you and help you.

JOHN 15:16; PHILIPPIANS 2:13; ISAIAH 41:10

*Lord, what can I pray when I'm ready for
you to work through me?*

Now all glory to you, God, who is able, through your
mighty power at work within me, to accomplish infinitely more than I might ask or think. Glory to you in
the church and in Christ Jesus through all generations
forever and ever!   EPHESIANS 3:20-21

*Don't allow your limitations or inexperience to keep you from
serving God. When you feel discouraged or inadequate, remember
that God often uses ordinary people to accomplish extraordinary
things. Instead of doubting God's decision to use you, step out in
faith and trust that he is able to carry out his plans through you.
Find further encouragement by reading the stories of David
(1 Samuel 17), Mary (Luke 1), and Gideon (Judges 6).*

30

IS THE PRESSURE GETTING TO YOU?

Lord, what is an example from your Word of someone being overcome by the pressures of life?

Moses said, "When a dispute arises, the people come to me, and I am the one who settles the case between the quarreling parties. I inform the people of God's decrees and give them his instructions." "This is not good!" Moses' father-in-law exclaimed. "You're going to wear yourself out—and the people, too. This job is too heavy a burden for you to handle all by yourself."

EXODUS 18:15-18

What can I do when a burden is too much to carry all by myself?

Select some capable, honest individuals who fear me and will help you carry the load, making the task easier for you. If you follow this advice, you will be able to endure the pressures. But you must build each other up in your most holy faith, pray in the power of the Holy Spirit, and await the mercy of your Lord Jesus

Christ, who will bring you eternal life. In this way, you will keep yourselves safe in my love.

EXODUS 18:21-23; JUDE 1:20-21

What can I pray when I'm under pressure?
Do not stay so far from me, LORD, for trouble is near, and no one else can help me. O LORD, do not stay far away! You are my strength; come quickly to my aid! Hear me, LORD, and have mercy on me. Help me, O LORD.   PSALM 22:11, 19; PSALM 30:10

Are you in a season where the demands of life are far too much for you to handle? Moses' father-in-law gave good advice: Delegate and ask for help! If you are feeling burdened, ask someone for assistance. Can you delegate a task at work? Can you ask your spouse or a child for help around the house? Is there a friend who can come over and lighten your load?

31

YOU DON'T NEED TO WORRY: TRUST GOD

Lord, I feel anxious about the future. How can I trust you to take care of me?

Don't worry about everyday life, saying, "What will I eat? What will I drink? What will I wear?" These things dominate the thoughts of unbelievers, but I already know all your needs. Seek my Kingdom above all else, and live righteously, and I will give you everything you need.   MATTHEW 6:31-33

What does your Word tell me to do when I feel anxiety begin to take over?

Don't worry about anything; instead, pray about everything. Tell me what you need, and thank me for all I have done. Then you will experience my peace, which exceeds anything you can understand. My peace will guard your heart and mind as you live in Christ Jesus. I am close to all who call on me; yes, to all who call on me in truth.   PHILIPPIANS 4:6-7; PSALM 145:18

What can I pray when I am anxious?

Search me, O God, and know my heart; test me and know my anxious thoughts. Point out anything in me that offends you, and lead me along the path of everlasting life.   PSALM 139:23-24

God promises to take care of those who trust him and stay close to him. Make a list of the things you feel anxious about this evening. Keep this list tucked in your Bible or in a safe place to remind you to pray whenever you feel anxious thoughts creep in. Pray that God will transform your anxious heart into one that trusts him to take care of each and every item on your list.

UNITY THROUGH DIVERSITY

Lord, how can I find unity with others
who are so different?

Make every effort to keep yourselves united in the
Spirit, binding yourselves together with peace. Always
be humble and gentle. Be patient with each other,
making allowance for each other's faults because of
your love. If you love only those who love you, what
reward is there for that? If you are kind only to your
friends, how are you different from anyone else? Even
pagans do that. But you are to be perfect, even as I
am perfect.

EPHESIANS 4:3; EPHESIANS 4:2;
MATTHEW 5:46-48

What can I remember when my differences
with others cause frustration?

Just as your body has many parts and each part has a
special function, so it is with my body. Christians are
many parts of one body, and you all belong to each

other. In my grace, I have given you different gifts for doing certain things well.   ROMANS 12:4-6

What can I pray when differences bring conflict?
Father God, who gives me patience and encouragement, help me live in complete harmony with others, so that we can join together with one voice, giving praise and glory to you, the Father of our Lord Jesus Christ.   ROMANS 15:5-6

God has woven diversity into his creation. Therefore we should expect differences of opinion. Unity is not everyone agreeing— it's learning how to take different thoughts and direct them all toward a shared purpose and goal. Think of someone whose life is different from yours. What good qualities does he or she have? What is something you could learn from him or her? Spend a moment thanking God for the rich blessing of diversity he has created in the world, and ask him if there is someone specific he wants you to seek unity with.

THE WAY TO
A HARD HEART

Lord, what can cause my heart to wander from you?
Do not love this world nor the things it offers you, for
when you love the world, you do not have my love in
you. For the world offers only a craving for physical
pleasure, a craving for everything you see, and pride
in your achievements and possessions. Make sure that
your own heart is not evil and unbelieving, turning
you away from me. Beware that in your plenty you
do not forget me and disobey my commands, regulations, and decrees that I have given you.

1 JOHN 2:15-16; HEBREWS 3:12;
2 CORINTHIANS 11:3; DEUTERONOMY 8:11

*What should I do when I feel hard-hearted
and rebellious?*
Today when you hear my voice, don't harden your
heart against me as Israel did when they rebelled,
when they tested me in the wilderness. If you want
to return to me, you can. You can throw away your

detestable idols and stray away no more. My wayward child, come back to me, and I will heal your wayward heart. Keep on doing what is right, and trust your life to the God who created you, for I will never fail you.

HEBREWS 3:7-8; JEREMIAH 4:1; JEREMIAH 3:22; I PETER 4:19

What can I pray to keep my heart from wandering?
Once I was like a sheep who wandered away. But now I have turned to you, my Shepherd, the Guardian of my soul. I PETER 2:25

The heart is a fickle thing, easily deceived to doubt that God's ways are best. When life is going well, your heart can be tempted to forget its need for God. But through Christ, there is always a way to return to closeness with God and have your heart softened once again. Close your eyes and breathe deeply. Pay attention to the sound of your heartbeat. Relax and breathe, inviting God to soften your heart toward him in this moment.

LET YOUR
GOOD DEEDS SHINE

Lord, what do good deeds say about my faith?
What good is it if you say you have faith but don't show
it by your actions? Can that kind of faith save anyone?
Suppose you see a brother or sister who has no food or
clothing, and you say, "Good-bye and have a good day;
stay warm and eat well"—but then you don't give that
person any food or clothing. What good does that do?
So you see, faith by itself isn't enough. Unless it produces good deeds, it is dead and useless.

JAMES 2:14-17

How do my actions affect those around me?
You are the light of the world—like a city on a hilltop
that cannot be hidden. No one lights a lamp and then
puts it under a basket. Instead, a lamp is placed on a
stand, where it gives light to everyone in the house.
Let your good deeds shine out for all to see, so that
everyone will praise me.   MATTHEW 5:14-16

*What can I pray when I want my good
deeds to shine for you?*

Oh, that my actions would consistently reflect your
decrees! Then I will not be ashamed when I compare
my life with your commands. As I learn your righteous
regulations, I will thank you by living as I should!

PSALM 119:5-7

Is your life a recommendation to follow Jesus? If people were to look
at the way you live, would it be obvious that you follow Christ?
Would your actions inspire others to want more of Jesus in their lives?

LEARNING TO FORGIVE YOURSELF

*Lord, if I can't forgive myself for my mistakes,
how could you forgive me?*
Come now, let's settle this. Though your sins are
like scarlet, I will make them as white as snow.
Though they are red like crimson, I will make
them as white as wool. I—yes, I alone—will
blot out your sins for my own sake and will
never think of them again.

ISAIAH 1:18; ISAIAH 43:25; ISAIAH 1:5

But Lord, what if I've done some really horrible things?
Healthy people don't need a doctor—sick people
do. I have come to call not those who think they
are righteous, but those who know they are sinners. Fear not; you will no longer live in shame.
Don't be afraid; there is no more disgrace for you.
There is no condemnation for those who belong
to Christ Jesus. So rejoice in me and be glad, all
you who obey me! Shout for joy, all you whose

hearts are pure! Yes, what joy for those whose record
I have cleared of guilt.

MARK 2:17; ISAIAH 54:4; ROMANS 8:1;
PSALM 32:11; PSALM 32:2

How can I express my gratitude for
your forgiveness in prayer?
You forgave me! All my guilt is gone. In you my
heart rejoices, for I trust in your holy name.

PSALM 32:5; PSALM 33:21

It can feel incredibly difficult to forgive yourself for the mistakes you have made, especially when you see the impact of those choices. But forgiveness is one of the greatest gifts God has given us. What is one mistake from your past that makes it hard to receive forgiveness? Read 2 Corinthians 5:17 as a reminder of how God sees you after you have been forgiven.

JUST BE YOU

Lord, how can I stop comparing myself to others?
Pay careful attention to your own work, for then
you will get the satisfaction of a job well done,
and you won't need to compare yourself to anyone
else. For you are responsible for your own conduct.
I have given people different gifts for doing certain
things well. Think about the things of heaven, not
the things of earth. Do this by keeping your eyes
on Jesus, the champion who initiates and perfects
your faith.

GALATIANS 6:4-5; ROMANS 12:6; COLOSSIANS 3:2;
HEBREWS 12:2

*What is an example of unhealthy versus
healthy comparison?*
The Pharisee stood by himself and prayed this prayer:
"I thank you, God, that I am not like other people—
cheaters, sinners, adulterers. I fast twice a week, and I
give you a tenth of my income." But the tax collector
stood at a distance and dared not even lift his eyes
to heaven as he prayed. Instead, he beat his chest in

sorrow, saying, "O God, be merciful to me, for I am a sinner." LUKE 18:11-13

What can I pray when I feel tempted to compare my life to someone else's?
Let all that I am praise you, LORD; with my whole heart, I will praise your holy name. Let all that I am praise you, LORD; may I never forget the good things you do for me. PSALM 103:1-2

When we look to others for who we should or shouldn't be, it either leads to pride, as it did with the Pharisee, or it makes us feel inferior. We are meant to look to the Lord. Where do you feel most tempted to compare yourself to others? Write a list of the ways God has shown you his mercy, blessed you, and called you to be unique.

LIVING A FRUITFUL LIFE

Lord, how does the Bible help me grow in my faith?
The rain and snow come down from the heavens and
stay on the ground to water the earth. They cause
the grain to grow, producing seed for the farmer and
bread for the hungry. It is the same with my word.
I send it out, and it always produces fruit. It will
accomplish all I want it to, and it will prosper everywhere I send it. ISAIAH 55:10-11

*What is the spiritual fruit that results from
being nourished by your Word?*
The Holy Spirit produces this kind of fruit in your life:
love, joy, peace, patience, kindness, goodness, faithfulness, gentleness, and self-control. The wisdom from
above is first of all pure. It is also peace loving, gentle
at all times, and willing to yield to others. It is full of
mercy and the fruit of good deeds. It shows no favoritism and is always sincere. And those who are peace-
makers will plant seeds of peace and reap a harvest of
righteousness. GALATIANS 5:22-23; JAMES 3:17-18

What can I pray before I open your Word?
May I always be filled with the fruit of my salvation—
the righteous character produced in my life by Jesus
Christ—for this will bring much glory and praise
to you.   PHILIPPIANS 1:11

Reading the Bible grows your faith and nourishes your heart, even when you don't feel it. God has given you his Word to bring about abundant life, fruitfulness, and spiritual maturity. It is a gift always ready to be received. Reflect on the times when God's Word has been fruitful in your life. How can you put yourself in situations or around people who encourage you to grow in your knowledge of God's Word?

YOU AREN'T ALONE
IN THE PIT OF GRIEF

Lord, is there something wrong with me if I'm still feeling sad long after a great loss?

For everything there is a season. A time to cry and a time to laugh. A time to grieve and a time to dance. When you go through deep waters, I will be with you. When you go through rivers of difficulty, you will not drown. Do not be afraid, for I am with you. Here on earth you will have many trials and sorrows. But take heart, because I have overcome the world.

ECCLESIASTES 3:1, 4; ISAIAH 43:2, 5; JOHN 16:33

How do you come alongside me in my grief?

I am close to the brokenhearted; I rescue those whose spirits are crushed. And the Holy Spirit helps you in your weakness. For example, you don't know what I want you to pray for. But the Holy Spirit prays for you with groanings that cannot be expressed in words. PSALM 34:18; ROMANS 8:26

What can I pray in my moments of grief?

You keep track of all my sorrows. You have collected all my tears in your bottle. You have recorded each one in your book. Now let your unfailing love comfort me, just as you promised me. Lord, your faithful love never ends! Your mercies never cease. Great is your faithfulness; your mercies begin afresh each morning.

PSALM 56:8; PSALM 119:76; LAMENTATIONS 3:22-23

God doesn't give us a timeline for getting over our grief. But when sorrow becomes a part of our story, he promises to comfort us. Deep grief over a loss shows how deeply you allowed yourself to love. When it is time, God will begin to create space in your heart so you can embrace the next chapter in life. Until then, allow yourself the time to grieve. Reread the verses above to remind yourself that God is with you and is comforting you in your pain.

GOD IS PREPARING A PLACE FOR YOU

Lord, is heaven a reality I can count on?

I want to remind you that in the last days scoffers will come, mocking the truth and following their own desires. They will say, "What happened to the promise that Jesus is coming again?" But you are looking forward to the new heavens and new earth I have promised, a world filled with my righteousness. There is more than enough room in my home, and I am going to prepare a place for you.

2 PETER 3:3-4, 13; JOHN 14:2

But where is heaven?

Then the apostle John saw a new heaven and a new earth, for the old heaven and the old earth had disappeared. And the sea was also gone. And he saw the holy city, the new Jerusalem, coming down from me out of heaven like a bride beautifully dressed for her husband. He heard a loud shout from my throne, saying, "Look, my home is now among my people! I will live with them, and they will be my people. I myself will be with them." REVELATION 21:1-3

What can I pray as I think about
your promise of heaven?
Father, no eye has seen, no ear has heard, and no mind has imagined what you have prepared for those who love you. But you revealed these things by your Spirit. For your Spirit searches out everything and shows us your deep secrets.   I CORINTHIANS 2:9-10

The Bible speaks of a new heaven and a new earth, a re-creation and restoration of the universe, coinciding with Jesus' return. When the new heaven and earth come, God's home will be with his people. Close your eyes and picture the moment when God's promise is fulfilled and you see Jesus face-to-face. What emotions arise in you as you realize you are finally home?

LOVE YOUR SPOUSE LIKE THIS

Lord, what is your vision for marriage?

A man leaves his father and mother and is joined to his wife, and the two are united into one. Give honor to marriage, and remain faithful to one another in marriage. And further, submit to one another out of reverence for Christ. For wives, this means submit to your husbands as to the Lord. For husbands, this means love your wives, just as Christ loved the church.

EPHESIANS 5:31; HEBREWS 13:4;
EPHESIANS 5:21-22, 25

What is the one thing that will keep a marriage together?

Above all, clothe yourselves with love, which binds us all together in perfect harmony. Love is patient and kind. Love is not jealous or boastful or proud or rude. It does not demand its own way. It is not irritable, and it keeps no record of being wronged.

COLOSSIANS 3:14; I CORINTHIANS 13:4-5

What can I pray over my marriage?

Make my love for others and for all people grow and overflow, just as your love for me overflows.

I THESSALONIANS 3:12

God designed marriage to bring us joy, intimacy, and companionship. However, he also intended for it to be refining, to help each spouse grow in holiness and in the love and likeness of Jesus. Transformation often happens through the tough parts of marriage—sacrifice, forgiveness, and grace. The rewards of a strong marriage are worth the hard work. Spend time meditating on Ephesians 5:21-22 and 1 Corinthians 13:4-7 while praying for your marriage to reflect the love these passages illustrate. As you read, what stands out to you? Is there anything convicting? In what area would you like to see you and your spouse become more united?

STAY CONNECTED TO THE SPIRIT

Lord, what does it mean to be filled with your Spirit?
When you believed in me, I identified you as my own
by giving you the Holy Spirit, whom I promised long
ago. The Spirit is my guarantee that I will give you
the inheritance I promised and that I have purchased
you to be mine. I did this so you would praise and
glorify me. The Holy Spirit produces this kind of fruit
in your life: love, joy, peace, patience, kindness, goodness, faithfulness, gentleness, and self-control.

EPHESIANS 1:13-14; GALATIANS 5:22-23

*If I have your Spirit in me, why do I still
struggle to do what's right?*
You want to do what is right, but you can't. You want
to do what is good, but you don't. You don't want to
do what is wrong, but you do it anyway. But if you
do what you don't want to do, you are not really the
one doing wrong; it is sin living in you that does it.
The sinful nature wants to do evil, which is just the

opposite of what the Spirit wants. And the Spirit gives you desires that are the opposite of what the sinful nature desires. These two forces are constantly fighting each other, so you are not free to carry out your good intentions. ROMANS 7:18-20; GALATIANS 5:17

What can I pray when I doubt the Holy Spirit's presence?
I have received your Spirit (not the world's spirit), so I can know the wonderful things you have freely given me. For your Spirit joins with my spirit to affirm that I am your child. Thank you, God, that I can never escape from your Spirit!

I CORINTHIANS 2:12; ROMANS 8:16; PSALM 139:7

Have you ever tried to hold together two magnets with the same polarity? It's impossible. The two forces repel one another. Likewise, what your sinful nature craves opposes your connection with the Holy Spirit, because your sinful nature is still vying for control over your desires. That's why it's so important to submit to the Holy Spirit's work. He helps change your desires to those that please him.

THE WAY TO SECURE UNFADING BEAUTY

Lord, how much should I invest in my outward appearance?

Don't be concerned about the outward beauty of fancy hairstyles, expensive jewelry, or beautiful clothes. You must clothe yourself with tenderhearted mercy, kindness, humility, gentleness, and patience—the beauty that comes from within, the unfading beauty of a gentle and quiet spirit, which is so precious to me. People judge by outward appearance, but I look at the heart. I—the Spirit—make you more and more like Jesus as you are changed into his glorious image.

I PETER 3:3; COLOSSIANS 3:12; I PETER 3:4;
I SAMUEL 16:7; 2 CORINTHIANS 3:18

How can I have a heart that reflects your beauty, Lord?

When Moses came down Mount Sinai carrying the two stone tablets inscribed with the terms of the covenant, he wasn't aware that his face had become radiant because he had spoken to me. I reveal my holiness through you. Remain in me, and I will remain in you.

EXODUS 34:29; EZEKIEL 36:23; JOHN 15:4

What can I pray to better reflect your beauty?
Make your light shine in my heart so I can know the glory that is seen in the face of Jesus Christ.

2 CORINTHIANS 4:6

Developing a beautiful character is an investment of unfading value. Moses was radiant because he spent time in the presence of God. The more connected you are to the Lord, the more your heart will reflect his heart. How much time do you invest in your physical appearance each day? What if you spent the same amount of time working on improving your character? How can you carve out extra time this evening to be with Jesus and invest in growing your inner beauty?

DON'T REMAIN STAGNANT

Lord, what does your Word say about apathy?

You are neither hot nor cold. I wish you were one or the other! But since you are like lukewarm water, I will spit you out of my mouth! To whom can I give warning? Who will listen when I speak? Don't drift away. Anyone who isn't helping me opposes me, and anyone who isn't working with me is actually working against me.

REVELATION 3:15-16; JEREMIAH 6:10;
COLOSSIANS 1:23; MATTHEW 12:30

What are some practical ways I can fight against apathy?

You say, "It's too hard to serve the LORD," and you turn up your nose at my commands. My child, never forget the things I have taught you. Store my commands in your heart. If you do this, your life will be satisfying. But you must continue to believe this truth and stand firmly in it. Keep on loving others as long as life lasts. Then you will not become spiritually dull and indifferent.

MALACHI 1:13; PROVERBS 3:1-2;
COLOSSIANS 1:23; HEBREWS 6:11-12

*What can I pray when I want a renewed
passion for you, Lord?*
O God, you are my God; I earnestly search for you. Whom have I in heaven but you? I desire you more than anything on earth. PSALM 63:1; PSALM 73:25

Today, choose to step toward God, even when you don't feel like it. He can use your weakest yes to bring revival to your heart. Write down some small and achievable goals for this week, this month, and this year that will help your heart reconnect with the Lord. Prayerfully consider goals that focus on finding ways to awaken your heart to the love and presence of God, such as reading God's Word and loving and serving others.

GOD DOESN'T CREATE MISTAKES

Lord, sometimes I don't like who I am.
Why did you create me this way?

Does a clay pot argue with its maker? Does the clay dispute with the one who shapes it, saying, "Stop, you're doing it wrong!" I knew you before I formed you in your mother's womb. Before you were born I set you apart. Not a single sparrow can fall to the ground without my knowing it. And you are more valuable to me than a whole flock of sparrows.

ISAIAH 45:9; JEREMIAH 1:5;
MATTHEW 10:29-31

How can I value myself the way you do?

You are my masterpiece. I have created you anew in Christ Jesus, so you can do the good things I planned for you long ago. Even before I made the world, I loved you and chose you in Christ to be holy and without fault in my eyes. I decided in advance to adopt you into my own family by bringing you to myself through Jesus Christ. This is what I wanted to do, and it gave me great pleasure.

EPHESIANS 2:10; EPHESIANS 1:4-5

What can I pray when my self-esteem is low?
How precious are your thoughts about me, O God. They cannot be numbered! PSALM 139:17

Our self-esteem flourishes when we can see ourselves the way God sees us. Instead of focusing on your flaws, reflect on what your creator says about your worth. Write down a few lies or negative thoughts Satan tempts you to believe about yourself. Now reflect on the words God uses to describe you: loved, valuable, precious, a masterpiece, and my child. How might you see yourself if you let go of the lies and instead chose to live out how God sees you?

WHAT REAL LOVE
LOOKS LIKE

Lord, what is your ideal for love?

Love is patient and kind. Love is not jealous or boastful or proud or rude. It does not demand its own way. It is not irritable, and it keeps no record of being wronged. It does not rejoice about injustice but rejoices whenever the truth wins out. Love never gives up, never loses faith, is always hopeful, and endures through every circumstance.   I CORINTHIANS 13:4-7

How is this kind of love even possible?

You know how dearly I love you, because I have given you the Holy Spirit to fill your heart with my love. You love others because I loved you first. I am love, and all who live in love live in me, and I live in them. And as you live in me, your love grows more perfect.

ROMANS 5:5; I JOHN 4:19; I JOHN 4:16-17

How can I pray when I want to love others as you do?
With all my heart I will praise you, O Lord my God.
I will give glory to your name forever, for your love
for me is very great. May you make my love for other
Christians and for all people grow and overflow, just
as your love for me overflows.

PSALM 86:12-13; I THESSALONIANS 3:12

*Jesus is our example of real love. In everything he did, he was
patient, kind, humble, peaceful, faithful, and had the heart of a
servant. His love endured the cross, taking the penalty for our
sin upon himself. His love gives us hope because it was strong
enough to defeat death and give us the means to receive God's
love forever. In light of what Jesus has done for you in love, choose
someone to love today by asking, "What can I do for you?"
When you follow through, thank God for how he loves you.*

DEVELOPING A DEEPER RELATIONSHIP WITH GOD

Lord, how do you pursue an intimate relationship with me?

Even before I made the world, I loved you and chose you in Christ to be holy and without fault in my eyes. I showed my great love for you by sending Christ to die for you while you were still a sinner. So now you can rejoice in your wonderful new relationship with me because your Lord Jesus Christ has made you a friend of mine.   EPHESIANS 1:4; ROMANS 5:8, 11

How am I to pursue an intimate relationship with you?

I am close to all who call on me; yes, to all who call on me in truth. You must love me with all your heart, all your soul, and all your mind. You must worship no other gods, for I am jealous about my relationship with you.

PSALM 145:18; MATTHEW 22:37; EXODUS 34:14

What can I pray to remember that your intimate love is always available to me?

Each day, you pour your unfailing love upon me, LORD, and through each night I sing your songs, praying to you, God, who gives me life.

PSALM 42:8

*I*ntimacy happens through knowing and being known by someone. We can know things about God that he has revealed through his Word and through experience, but we must also open our hearts to be known by him. Prayerfully consider whether you are open to God in your heart, mind, and spirit. Is there anything preventing you from drawing nearer to him in any of these areas? Examples might be fear, doubt, addictions, fantasies, trauma, selfishness, or pride. Invite the Lord into these areas of your life and tell him you are ready to open all of yourself to a deeper relationship with him.

OBEDIENCE IS
FOR YOUR BLESSING

Lord, why do you command my obedience?
Do what is right and good in my sight, so all will
go well with you. I commanded you to obey all my
decrees and to fear me so I can continue to bless you
and preserve your life. Those who obey my commands remain in fellowship with me, and I with
them. When you obey my commandments, you
remain in my love.

DEUTERONOMY 6:18, 24; 1 JOHN 3:24;
JOHN 15:10

What are some of the blessings of obedience?
Oh, the joys of those who do not follow the advice
of the wicked, or stand around with sinners, or join
in with mockers. They delight in my law, meditating on it day and night. They are like trees planted
along the riverbank, bearing fruit each season. Their
leaves never wither, and they prosper in all they do.
Obey me, and I will be your God, and you will be

my people. Do everything as I say, and all will
be well!   PSALM 1:1-3; JEREMIAH 7:23

*What can I pray to help me walk more
faithfully in obedience to you?*
I will not compromise with evil, LORD, and will walk
only in your paths. Oh, that my actions would consistently reflect your decrees! Then I will not be ashamed
when I compare my life with your commands. As I
learn your righteous regulations, I will thank you by
living as I should!   PSALM 119:3, 5-7

*Your obedience to God is proof of your love for him and your
desire to remain close to him. Obedience also opens up pathways
of blessing. Reflect on this past year. When have you practiced
obedience to God? Where have you seen the fruit or blessing
of that obedience? Say a prayer of thankfulness to God for
giving you commands that protect and bless you.*

WHAT TO DO WHEN SOMEONE HURTS YOU

Lord, do I really need to be kind to someone who isn't kind to me?

You have heard that the law says, "Love your neighbor" and hate your enemy. But I say, love your enemies! Pray for those who persecute you! In that way, you will be acting as true children of mine.

MATTHEW 5:43-45

But how can I possibly love or pray for someone who has hurt me?

Never take revenge. Leave that to my righteous anger. I will take revenge; I will pay them back. Instead, if your enemies are hungry, feed them. If they are thirsty, give them something to drink. Don't let evil conquer you, but conquer evil by doing good. Be careful to live properly among your unbelieving neighbors. Then even if they accuse you of doing wrong, they will see your honorable behavior, and they will give honor to me when I judge the world.   ROMANS 12:19-21; 1 PETER 2:12

What can I pray for those who have hurt me?

Father, forgive them, for they don't know what they are doing.   LUKE 23:34

If there is someone in your life who seems impossible to love, begin by praying, "Lord, how do you want me to pray for this person?" Prayer keeps your focus on God and off retaliation or self-pity. Over time, God can change the posture of your heart toward this person. Whenever you feel hurt, pray. Whenever you feel betrayed, pray. Whenever you feel heartbroken, pray. Start praying for your enemies tonight. How can you remind yourself to continue to pray for them?

PAIN CULTIVATES YOUR HOPE FOR HEALING

Lord, what is the best perspective in dealing with physical pain?

Even though you have the Holy Spirit within you as a foretaste of future glory, you long for your body to be released from sin and suffering. You wait with eager hope for the day when I will give you your full rights as my adopted child, including the new body I have promised you.   ROMANS 8:23

How can I have an eternal perspective in the midst of my pain?

Since Christ suffered physical pain, you must arm yourselves with the same attitude he had, and be ready to suffer, too. For if you have suffered physically for Christ, you have finished with sin. You won't spend the rest of your life chasing your own desires, but you will be anxious to do my will. That is why you never give up. Though your body is dying, your spirit is being renewed every day. For your present troubles are small and won't last very long. Yet they produce for you a glory that vastly outweighs them and will last forever! I PETER 4:1-2; 2 CORINTHIANS 4:16-17

When the pain is overwhelming, how should I pray?
I am on the verge of collapse, facing constant pain. Do not abandon me, O LORD. Do not stand at a distance, my God. Come quickly to help me, O Lord my savior. PSALM 38:17, 21-22

Close your eyes and try to focus on the parts of your body that aren't in pain. Go through each part and praise God for the areas that aren't hurting. Thank him for the promise that in heaven, your whole body will be pain free. Ask him to renew your spirit to face each day.

WHAT DO YOU TREASURE?

Lord, what does idolatry look like in this day and age?
Dear child, keep away from anything that might take
my place in your heart. Ever since the world was created, people have clearly seen my invisible qualities—
my eternal power and divine nature. Yes, they knew
me, but they wouldn't worship me as God or even
give me thanks. Instead, they worshiped idols and
served the things I created.

I JOHN 5:21; ROMANS 1:20-21, 23, 25

How do I begin to identify the idols in my heart?
Wherever your treasure is, there the desires of your heart
will also be. Don't store up treasures here on earth. Store
your treasures in heaven, where moths and rust cannot
destroy, and thieves do not break in and steal. Come
back to me, and I will heal your wayward hearts. Wash
your hands, you sinners; purify your hearts, for your
loyalty is divided between me and the world.

MATTHEW 6:21; MATTHEW 6:19-20; JEREMIAH 3:22;
JAMES 4:8

What can I pray when I need to turn my
heart back to you?

Let me worship and bow down. Let me kneel before
the LORD my maker. For you, O LORD, are supreme
over all the earth; you are exalted far above all gods.

PSALM 95:6; PSALM 97:9

*Loving the gifts of God more than the giver himself is idolatry.
It is only when you recognize and acknowledge the idols in your life
that you can be set free from them. What things have replaced
your desire for God? Confess this to the Lord and take the first step
toward receiving his mercy. Repeatedly seeking after God
will make him the primary thing your heart desires.*

WHEN YOU'RE CALLED OUT OF YOUR COMFORT ZONE

Lord, will you ever call me to do something that seems risky?

I said to Abram, "Leave your native country, your relatives, and your father's family, and go to the land that I will show you." I said to Moses, "Now go, for I am sending you to Pharaoh. You must lead my people Israel out of Egypt."

GENESIS 12:1; EXODUS 3:10

How can I find the courage to follow you even in uncertainty?

Anyone who wants to come to me must believe that I exist and that I reward those who sincerely seek me. It was by faith that Abraham obeyed when I called him to leave home and go to another land that I would give him as his inheritance. He went without knowing where he was going. And even when he reached the land I promised him, he lived there by faith. Abraham was confidently looking forward to a city with eternal foundations, a city designed and built by me.

HEBREWS 11:6, 8-10

What can I pray to find the courage to follow you despite the risks?

Lord, you are my light and my salvation—so why should I be afraid? You are my fortress, protecting me from danger, so why should I tremble? PSALM 27:1

In C. S. Lewis's classic book The Lion, the Witch and the Wardrobe, *the character Susan asks Mr. Beaver about Aslan, the king of Narnia, "Is he—quite safe? I shall feel rather nervous about meeting a lion."...."Safe?" said Mr. Beaver. "... Who said anything about safe? 'Course he isn't safe. But he's good."[4] What is the one thing that holds you back from taking risks for God? Pray Psalm 27:1 for courage to follow God no matter the risk.*

CREATED
FOR GREAT THINGS

Lord, I often feel nondescript and ordinary.
Do you even know I'm here?

I knew you before I formed you in your mother's womb. Before you were born I set you apart. I am watching, and I will certainly carry out all my plans. For I know the plans I have for you. They are plans for good and not for disaster, to give you a future and a hope.   JEREMIAH 1:5, 12; JEREMIAH 29:11

How can I start living out this wonderful
plan you have for me?

If you look for me wholeheartedly, you will find me. I will be found by you. Remain faithful to the things you have been taught—the holy Scriptures. They have given you the wisdom to receive the salvation that comes by trusting in Christ Jesus. Pray in the Spirit at all times and on every occasion. Stay alert and be persistent in your prayers for all believers everywhere.

JEREMIAH 29:13-14; 2 TIMOTHY 3:14-15;
EPHESIANS 6:18

What can I pray when I feel uninspired?

God, in your grace, you freely make me right in your sight. With your help, I will do mighty things. For I am your masterpiece. You have created me anew in Christ Jesus, so I can do the good things you planned for me long ago.

ROMANS 3:24; PSALM 60:12; EPHESIANS 2:10

No matter how ordinary and insignificant you feel, God's Word affirms that you are special and have purpose—that you are God's masterpiece. Look at a classic work of art. Notice the intricate details and how the art reveals so much about its creator. Think about how that piece has influenced people across time. That captures the essence of how important and valuable you are to God. How does this perspective empower you? What is one good thing you can do as God's masterpiece that will reveal the Creator to someone else?

WHY TRUTH MATTERS

Lord, with so much access to information, how can I know what is really true?

The very essence of my words is truth; all my just regulations will stand forever. I was born and came into the world to testify to the truth. All who love the truth recognize that what I say is true.

PSALM 119:160; JOHN 18:37

Lord Jesus, why is being able to recognize the truth so important?

I am the way, the truth, and the life. No one can come to the Father except through me. This truth gives you confidence that you have eternal life, which I promised before the world began—and I do not lie.   JOHN 14:6; TITUS 1:2

What can I pray when I need you to guide me to the truth?

Open my eyes to see the wonderful truths in your instructions. Lead me by your truth and teach me, for you are the God who saves me. All day long I put my hope in you.   PSALM 119:18; PSALM 25:5

A predominant view today is that we can create our own truth. This contradicts God's Word. Truth comes from God, who is the ultimate authority, who created everything and is sovereign over all that exists. His Word guides us into what is true and right. Set aside some time this evening to immerse yourself in Scripture. Start with Romans 1 and continue reading as long as you can. Pray that God will use this time to teach you to recognize what is true when you're faced with so many conflicting ideas.

ALLOW GOD'S WORD TO SINK IN

Lord, what does it mean to meditate on your Word?
Commit yourself wholeheartedly to these words
of mine. Tie them to your hands and wear them
on your forehead as reminders. Teach them to
your children. Talk about them when you are
at home and when you are on the road, when
you are going to bed and when you are getting
up. Show love to me by walking in my ways
and holding tightly to me. Study this Book of
Instruction continually. Meditate on it day and
night so you will be sure to obey everything
written in it.

DEUTERONOMY 11:18-19, 22; JOSHUA 1:8

*What will happen when I fill my thoughts
with your Word?*
When you discovered my words, you devoured them.
They are your joy and your heart's delight. Let the
message about Christ, in all its richness, fill your life.

I will keep in perfect peace all who trust in me, all whose thoughts are fixed on me.

JEREMIAH 15:16; COLOSSIANS 3:16; ISAIAH 26:3

*What can I pray to prepare my heart
before I read your Word?*
I will study your commandments and reflect on your ways. I ponder all your great works and think about what you have done. I will meditate on your majestic, glorious splendor and your wonderful miracles.

PSALM 119:15; PSALM 143:5; PSALM 145:5

What you put into your mind greatly influences your actions. How would your life be different if you thought about God's Word, his actions, and his presence throughout the day? Choose one verse to memorize and meditate on this week. When the verse comes to mind, take note of the time, place, or situation, and consider how it affects your actions.

OPEN YOURSELF UP TO
A DEEPER RELATIONSHIP

Lord, why is vulnerability so important?

As you share in others' sufferings, you will also share in
the comfort I give you. Confess your sins to each other
and pray for each other so that you may be healed. The
earnest prayer of a righteous person has great power
and produces wonderful results. Come boldly to my
throne of grace. There you will receive my mercy, and
you will find grace to help you when you need it most.

2 CORINTHIANS 1:7; JAMES 5:16; HEBREWS 4:16

What are the rewards of opening myself up to others?

Share each other's burdens, and in this way obey the law
of Christ. For where two or three gather together as my
followers, I am there among them. All of you should
be of one mind. Sympathize with each other. Love each
other as brothers and sisters. Be tenderhearted, and keep
a humble attitude. That is what I have called you to do,
and I will grant you my blessing.

GALATIANS 6:2; MATTHEW 18:20; 1 PETER 3:8-9

*What can I pray to encourage myself when
vulnerability seems hard?*

O LORD, you have examined my heart and know
everything about me. You know when I sit down or
stand up. You know my thoughts even when I'm far
away. You see me when I travel and when I rest at
home. You know everything I do. You know what I
am going to say even before I say it, LORD. You know
where I am going. And when you test me, I will come
out as pure as gold.   PSALM 139:1-4; JOB 23:10

*Vulnerability is sharing a personal struggle or confessing a sinful
habit you cannot defeat on your own. It's hard to show the weakest
parts of yourself to others. God's design is for believers to help and
strengthen each other. Do you have relationships like this? If not,
ask yourself if it's because you've been holding back. Who is someone
you want a deeper relationship with? What is something you
can share to allow this person to see a little more of you?*

GOD'S WAYS ARE SOMETIMES MYSTERIOUS

Lord, why do your ways seem so mysterious at times?
I am greater than you can understand. Just as you
cannot understand the path of the wind or the mystery of a tiny baby growing in its mother's womb,
so you cannot understand my activity. My ways are
far beyond anything you could imagine. For just as
the heavens are higher than the earth, so my ways
are higher than your ways and my thoughts higher
than your thoughts.

JOB 36:26; ECCLESIASTES 11:5; ISAIAH 55:8-9

What is a mystery you have revealed to me?
I want you to have complete confidence that you
understand my mysterious plan, which is Christ
himself. In him lie hidden all the treasures of wisdom and knowledge. At the right time I will bring
everything together under the authority of Christ—
everything in heaven and on earth. Furthermore,
because you are united with Christ, you have

received an inheritance from me, for I chose you in advance, and I make everything work out according to my plan.

COLOSSIANS 2:2-3; EPHESIANS 1:10-11

*What can I pray when I don't understand
what you are doing in my life?*
O God, my Savior, you work in mysterious ways. You will work out your plans for my life—for your faithful love, LORD, endures forever.

ISAIAH 45:15; PSALM 138:8

When we cannot make sense of a situation, it often makes us uncomfortable or distrusting. And when God acts in mysterious ways, it naturally challenges our faith. However, if God's nature and knowledge could be completely known by humans, we would cease to be in awe of him. God has given you all you need to know in order to believe in him. Take a moment to prayerfully ask, "Lord, what are you calling me to trust you with today?"

TAKE A LOAD OFF

*Lord, how can you help when my burdens
become too much?*

Give your burdens to me, and I will take care of you.
I will not permit the godly to slip and fall. I will take
the load from your shoulders; I will free your hands
from their heavy tasks. You cried to me in trouble,
and I saved you.   PSALM 55:22; PSALM 81:6-7

How can I live more freely and lightly in this season?
Stop at the crossroads and look around. Ask for the
old, godly way, and walk in it. Travel its path, and
you will find rest for your soul. Come to me, you
who are weary and carry heavy burdens, and I will
give you rest. Take my yoke upon you. Let me teach
you, because I am humble and gentle at heart, and
you will find rest for your soul. For my yoke is easy
to bear, and the burden I give you is light.

JEREMIAH 6:16; MATTHEW 11:28-30

What can I pray when I'm overwhelmed?

I give all my worries and cares to you, God, for you care about me.   I PETER 5:7

Are you carrying a heavy burden today? A faltering marriage? Sickness? Struggles at work? Disappointment with your children? Financial struggles? You were never meant to carry the full weight of these things. In prayer, picture lifting that burden off your shoulders and setting it down before the Lord. Ask him to remove the weight and carry it for you so you can have hope in this season.

STANDING STRONG IN THE FACE OF SETBACKS

Lord, can you encourage me in the face of this setback?
I have not given you a spirit of fear and timidity, but of power, love, and self-discipline. Be strong and courageous, and do the work. Don't be afraid or discouraged, for I am with you. I will not fail you or forsake you. Don't be dejected and sad, for my joy is your strength!

2 TIMOTHY 1:7; 1 CHRONICLES 28:20;
NEHEMIAH 8:10

What can encourage me?
How much more do I need to say? It would take too long to recount the stories of the faith of Gideon, Barak, Samson, Jephthah, David, Samuel, and all the prophets. By faith these people overthrew kingdoms, ruled with justice, and received what I had promised them. They shut the mouths of lions, quenched the flames of fire, and escaped death by the edge of the sword. Their weakness was turned

to strength. They became strong in battle and put whole armies to flight.　HEBREWS 11:32-34

What can I pray when I feel discouraged by a setback?
I know that you cause everything to work together for the good of those who love you and are called according to your purpose for them.　ROMANS 8:28

When it seems like a setback is keeping you from your dreams, read the full story of Joseph in Genesis 37–50. God has promised to use anything and everything for his good and ours. Looking at our setbacks from that perspective keeps us alert to what we can learn from them and the purpose that God will work out of them. Think of a setback you have faced in your life. How has God redeemed it? Has he allowed your setback to minister to others? Used your setback to shape you to become more like Jesus?

WHEN INTERRUPTIONS BECOME DIVINE APPOINTMENTS

Lord, how did Jesus handle interruptions in his ministry?

One day some parents brought their children to Jesus so he could lay his hands on them and pray for them. But the disciples scolded the parents for bothering him. But Jesus said, "Let the children come to me. Don't stop them! For the Kingdom of Heaven belongs to those who are like these children." And he placed his hands on their heads and blessed them before he left.

MATTHEW 19:13-15

When I'm interrupted, what should I be ready to do?

Don't forget to show hospitality to strangers, for some who have done this have entertained angels without realizing it! Be an example to all believers in what you say, in the way you live, in your love, your faith, and your purity. Look after each other so that none of you fails to receive my grace.

Watch out that no poisonous root of bitterness grows up to trouble you.

HEBREWS 13:2; I TIMOTHY 4:12; HEBREWS 12:15

What can I pray to handle life's interruptions with wisdom and grace?

Your wisdom from above is first of all pure. It is also peace loving, gentle at all times, and willing to yield to others. It is full of mercy and the fruit of good deeds. It shows no favoritism and is always sincere.

JAMES 3:17

Jesus always made time for people, even when they interrupted him. His disciples were frustrated by the little children, seeing them as a burden. But Jesus invited the children to come to him. How do you respond when others interrupt you? When people need your time or attention, are you resentful or welcoming of them? Whenever you're confronted by distractions or interruptions, stop and pray, "God, what is most important in this moment?" Try to see interruptions as divine appointments.

MERCY PAID FORWARD

Lord, how have you shown me mercy?

I am compassionate and merciful, slow to get angry and filled with unfailing love. I will not constantly accuse you, nor remain angry forever. I do not punish you for all your sins; I do not deal harshly with you, as you deserve. I am so rich in mercy, and I loved you so much, that even though you were dead because of your sins, I gave you life when I raised Christ from the dead. I saved you, not because of the righteous things you had done, but because of my mercy.

PSALM 103:8-10; EPHESIANS 2:4-5; TITUS 3:5

How should your mercy affect my daily life?

Since I chose you to be holy, you must clothe yourself with tenderhearted mercy, kindness, humility, gentleness, and patience. Make allowance for others' faults and forgive anyone who offends you. Remember, I forgave you, so you must forgive others.

COLOSSIANS 3:12-13

What can I pray to thank you for
your mercy in my life?

All praise to you, the Father of my Lord Jesus Christ.
It is by your great mercy that I have been born again,
because you raised Jesus Christ from the dead.

I PETER 1:3

Mercy is unmerited favor. Yet God's mercy goes a step further. He not only exempts you from the punishment for your sins, he also gives you the undeserved gift of salvation. Even more, God's mercies never end. It is by his mercy that your very life is sustained. Every breath is a merciful gift from an all-loving Father. Thank God for his mercies (breath in your lungs, safety for today, and salvation for eternity).

Then ask him who he wants you to be merciful to this week.

DEEPLY ROOTED

Lord, what is making me feel so unsettled?
The human heart is the most deceitful of all things,
and desperately wicked. Who really knows how bad it
is? Do not waver, for a person with divided loyalty is as
unsettled as a wave of the sea that is blown and tossed
by the wind. Such people should not expect to receive
anything from me. Their loyalty is divided between me
and the world, and they are unstable in everything they
do. If you are wise and understand my ways, prove it
by living an honorable life, doing good works with the
humility that comes from wisdom. Wickedness never
brings stability, but the godly have deep roots.

JEREMIAH 17:9; JAMES 1:6-8; JAMES 3:13;
PROVERBS 12:3

How do I grow strong and settled in my faith?
Be still in my presence, and wait patiently for me to act.
Put your hope in me. Travel steadily along my path.
Commit everything you do to me. Trust me, and I will
help you.   PSALM 37:7; PSALM 37:34; PSALM 37:5

What can I pray when I feel out of control?

Let my roots grow down into you, and let my life be built on you. Then my faith will grow strong in the truth I've been taught, and I will overflow with thankfulness. COLOSSIANS 2:7

When do you feel conflicted over competing desires? It is unsettling when your loyalties are at odds or divided. The Bible speaks about setting your mind and heart on the Lord. Committing your life to God and staying loyal to his commands makes you like a tree with deep roots, nurturing your faith to grow stronger and more stable. Take a "heart inventory" this evening. Do you feel deeply rooted? Or do you feel tossed about by waves of divided loyalty? Read the prayer again and choose in this moment to trust the Lord in the places where your desires are in conflict with his.

THE SOLUTION TO SIN

Lord, why was sin allowed to enter the world?
In the beginning I created the heavens and the earth.
Then I looked over all I had made, and I saw that it was
very good! When Adam sinned, sin entered the world.
Adam's sin brought death, so death spread to everyone,
for everyone sinned. Yes, Adam's one sin brings condemnation for everyone, but Christ's one act of righteousness brings a right relationship with me and new life for
everyone.   GENESIS 1:1, 31; ROMANS 5:12, 18

How can I combat sin and evil?
Put on all of my armor so that you will be able to
stand firm against all strategies of the devil. For you
are not fighting against flesh-and-blood enemies, but
against evil rulers and authorities of the unseen world.
You have already won a victory, because the Spirit who
lives in you is greater than the spirit who lives in the
world. For every child of mine defeats this evil world
through faith.

EPHESIANS 6:11-12; 1 JOHN 4:4; 1 JOHN 5:4

What can I pray over my home to declare God's glory and authority here?

All glory to you, God, who are able to keep me from falling away, and who will bring me with great joy into your glorious presence without a single fault. All glory to you, who alone are God, my Savior, through Jesus Christ my Lord. All glory, majesty, power, and authority are yours—beyond all time!

JUDE 1:24-25

Jesus is God's provision to end sin forever and to help you find freedom from the power of sin in your day-to-day life. Read the prayer above aloud to declare God's glory, majesty, power, and authority in your life and over your home this evening.

YOU DON'T NEED TO CLEAN YOURSELF UP FOR HIM

Lord, I feel like a mess. Does that make me unacceptable to you?

Jesus came to call not those who think they are righteous, but those who know they are sinners. For my way of making you right with me depends on faith. So now there is no condemnation for those who belong to Christ Jesus. If you openly declare that Jesus is Lord and believe in your heart that I raised him from the dead, you will be saved—and nothing in all creation will ever be able to separate you from my love that is revealed in Christ Jesus.

MARK 2:17; PHILIPPIANS 3:9; ROMANS 8:1; ROMANS 10:9; ROMANS 8:39

I believe you have forgiven me, but do you really accept me?

I saved you by my grace when you believed. This is a gift from me. Therefore, since you have been made right in my sight by faith, you have peace with me because of what Jesus Christ has done for you. Because of your faith, Christ has brought you into this place of undeserved privilege where you now stand, and you may confidently and joyfully look forward to sharing my glory.

EPHESIANS 2:8; ROMANS 5:1-2

What can I pray when I feel unworthy of
your acceptance?

I confessed all my sins to you and stopped trying to hide my guilt. I said to myself, "I will confess my rebellion to the LORD." And you forgave me! All my guilt is gone. PSALM 32:5

In this world, you must earn the acceptance of others. It isn't so with God. He accepts you not because of what you have done, but because of who you are—a precious child created in his image. As you sit before God in prayer, picture him seeing all of you—the good and the bad. Now see him opening his arms to embrace you. Breathe in his full acceptance, love, and grace. How would your days be different if you were confident of God's acceptance of you?

THE IMPORTANCE OF STAYING CONNECTED

Lord, what is the spiritual danger of constantly being connected to technology?

Don't copy the behavior and customs of this world, but let me transform you into a new person by changing the way you think. Then you will learn to know my will for you, which is good and pleasing and perfect. Fix your thoughts on what is true, and honorable, and right, and pure, and lovely, and admirable. Think about things that are excellent and worthy of praise.

ROMANS 12:2; PHILIPPIANS 4:8

What kind of boundaries should I have for technology and social media?

Guard your heart above all else, for it determines the course of your life. You say, "I am allowed to do anything"—but not everything is good for you. You say, "I am allowed to do anything"—but not everything is beneficial. So be careful how you live. Don't live like a fool, but like those who are wise. Make the most of every opportunity in these evil days.

PROVERBS 4:23; I CORINTHIANS 10:23;
EPHESIANS 5:15-16

*What can I pray to help me use technology
and social media well?*
I have received your Spirit (not the world's spirit), so I can know the wonderful things you have freely given me. So I say, let the Holy Spirit guide my life. Show me where to walk, for I give myself to you. Through the power of the Holy Spirit who lives within me, may I carefully guard the precious truth that has been entrusted to me.

I CORINTHIANS 2:12; GALATIANS 5:16;
PSALM 143:8; 2 TIMOTHY 1:14

Constant connection to technology can distract us, make us poor listeners, and compromise our ability to connect deeply with others. Assess your use of technology and how it affects your relationships. How can you more regularly detach from technology, especially social media, in order to be fully present with God and others?

GOD IS GOOD AND WANTS GOOD THINGS FOR YOU

Lord, how can I trust that you are good?

I am good to everyone. I shower compassion on all my creation. Whatever is good and perfect is a gift coming down to you from me, who created all the lights in the heavens. Don't you see how wonderfully kind, tolerant, and patient I am with you? Give thanks to me, for I am good! My faithful love endures forever. Taste and see that I am good. Oh, the joys of those who take refuge in me!

PSALM 145:9; JAMES 1:17; ROMANS 2:4;
I CHRONICLES 16:34; PSALM 34:8

How can I picture your Good News, Jesus?

I am the good shepherd. The good shepherd sacrifices his life for the sheep. I know my own sheep, and they know me, just as my Father knows me and I know him. So I sacrifice my life for the sheep. Yes, I am the gate. Those who come in through me will be saved. They will come and go freely and will find good pastures. The thief's purpose is to steal and kill and destroy. My purpose is to give them a rich and satisfying life. JOHN 10:11-15; JOHN 10:9-10

What can I pray when I need to be reminded of your goodness?

How great is the goodness you have stored up for those who fear you. You lavish it on those who come to you for protection, blessing them before the watching world. PSALM 31:19

When you truly love someone, you want only good for them. You give them good things. How much more does God, the giver of all good things, want to lavish his love upon you? Take a moment to prayerfully reflect on these two questions: When have you experienced God's goodness in your life? How might your days look different if you believed that God, who is absolutely good, desires good things for you?

BE CAREFUL WHAT
YOU LOOK AT

*Lord, does it really matter what I look at if
I'm not acting on it?*

The woman was convinced. She saw that the tree was
beautiful and its fruit looked delicious, and she wanted
the wisdom it would give her. So she took some of the
fruit and ate it. Then I asked the woman, "What have
you done?" GENESIS 3:6, 13

How can I be more intentional about what I look at?

If your eye causes you to sin, gouge it out and throw
it away. It's better to enter eternal life with only one
eye than to have two eyes and be thrown into the fire
of hell. Lift your eyes to me, your God, enthroned
in heaven. Keep looking to me for mercy. Fix your
thoughts on what is true, and honorable, and right,
and pure, and lovely, and admirable. Think about
things that are excellent and worthy of praise. Keep
putting into practice all you learned.

MATTHEW 18:9; PSALM 123:1-2; PHILIPPIANS 4:8-9

What can I pray to guide what I choose to look at?
I will be careful to live a blameless life—when will you come to help me? I will lead a life of integrity in my own home. I will refuse to look at anything vile and vulgar.   PSALM 101:2-3

What we allow ourselves to look at and linger on deeply affects our thoughts and actions. Take an inventory of the shows you watch, the books you read, the images you're allowing into your mind. What messages are you subtly allowing to influence you? Do they align with the truth from God's Word? What might be having the greatest influence on the way you think and act? Become intentional about filtering the images you allow into your eyes and mind.

THE BATTLE WITHIN YOU

Lord, why do I still have this inner conflict of wanting to please you while also wanting things that aren't pleasing to you?

You know that nothing good lives in you, that is, in your sinful nature. You want to do what is right, but you can't. You want to do what is good, but you don't. But if you do what you don't want to do, you are not really the one doing wrong; it is sin living in you that does it. ROMANS 7:18-20

How can I possibly overcome this inner conflict and truly desire to please you?

Who will free you from this life that is dominated by sin and death? The answer is in Jesus Christ. Adam's one sin brings condemnation for everyone, but Christ's one act of righteousness brings a right relationship with me and new life for everyone. So just as sin ruled over you and brought you to death, now my wonderful grace rules instead, giving you right standing with me and resulting in eternal life through Jesus Christ.

ROMANS 7:24-25; ROMANS 5:18, 21

*What can I pray as I struggle to have
victory over this conflict?*

O Lord, you are so good, so ready to forgive, so full
of unfailing love for all who ask for your help. I will
give glory to your name forever, for your love for me
is very great. You have rescued me from the depths
of death.   PSALM 86:5, 12-13

*The inner conflict we experience between desiring God but also
wanting and doing things we know aren't pleasing to him points
to the fact that God doesn't have our full loyalty yet. Since we are
believers in Jesus, sin no longer has the power to control us, but it
will still put up a good fight until Jesus comes again to rid the
world of sin forever. Until then, we fight an inner spiritual battle
every day. Do you sense this inner conflict in yourself? Read this
evening's prayer, allowing it to lead you to the one who provides
ultimate victory over sin and grace for today's mistakes.*

THE FREEDOM OF BOUNDARIES

Lord, why do I need boundaries?

Hide my word in your heart, that you might not sin against me. Walk along the path of my commands, for that is where your happiness is found. My commands make you wiser than your enemies, for my commands are your constant guide. I will guide your steps by my word, so you will not be overcome by evil.

PSALM 119:11, 35, 98, 133

What are some boundaries you set for me?

What do I, the LORD your God, require of you? I require only that you fear me, and live in a way that pleases me, and love me and serve me with all your heart and soul. You must always obey my commands and decrees that I have given you for your own good.

DEUTERONOMY 10:12-13

What can I pray to enjoy the safety and security of your boundaries?

You say that you will guide me along the best pathway for my life. You will advise me and watch over me. Help me not to be like a senseless horse or mule that needs a bit and bridle to keep it under control. Many sorrows come to the wicked, but unfailing love surrounds those who trust in you.   PSALM 32:8-10

God's boundaries are his loving restraints to keep you from falling away from him and the abundant life he offers. A guardrail on the road isn't there to restrict you but to keep you from danger. God's boundaries are designed to help you experience the blessings of his ways. Read the verses above as well as the Ten Commandments in Exodus 20:1-17. Which boundaries from God's Word are hard to accept? How would reframing your thinking from "This boundary is restrictive" to "This boundary is God's loving protection for me" affect the way you live?

WHEN YOU SEARCH FOR PEACE IN THE MIDDLE OF CHAOS

Lord, how can I find peace in my spirit when the world and my life seem to be in constant chaos?
I am the LORD your God. I created the heavens and earth and put everything in place. I made the world to be lived in, not to be a place of empty chaos. I am the LORD, and there is no other. I have told you all this so that you may have peace in me. Here on earth you will have many trials and sorrows. But take heart, because I have overcome the world.

ISAIAH 45:18; JOHN 16:33

How can you comfort me when chaos makes me afraid?
Do not fear when earthquakes come and the mountains crumble into the sea. Do not be afraid of the terrors of the night, nor the disaster that strikes at midday. No, do not be afraid, for I am

with you, and I am a great and awesome God.
I will comfort you as a mother comforts her child.

PSALM 46:2; PSALM 91:5-6; DEUTERONOMY 7:21;
ISAIAH 66:13

What can I pray to help me feel at peace?
You will keep me in perfect peace if I trust in you, if
my thoughts are fixed on you! In peace I will lie down
and sleep, for you alone, O LORD, will keep me safe.

ISAIAH 26:3; PSALM 4:8

Chaos can quickly replace our sense of peace with panic. We need to anchor our peace—not in present circumstances but in God, who is stable, steady, and sovereign over all things. Pause now. Close your eyes and breathe deeply. Relax your body and remind yourself that God is with you, that he is in control, and that he is a good and awesome God. As you take ten deep breaths, meditate on the image of God holding you safe.

YOU BELONG IN THE FAMILY OF GOD

Lord, what does it mean that I belong to you?
You have not received a spirit that makes you a fearful slave. Instead, you received my Spirit when I adopted you as my own child. Now you call me "Abba, Father." For my Spirit joins with your spirit to affirm that you are my child.   ROMANS 8:15-16

Jesus, what assurance do I have that I'm part of your family?
My sheep listen to my voice; I know them, and they follow me. I give them eternal life, and they will never perish. No one can snatch them away from me, for my Father has given them to me, and he is more powerful than anyone else. No one can snatch you from my Father's hand. For you are a child of God through your faith in me. And now that you belong to me, you are a true child of Abraham. You are among his heirs, and God's promise to Abraham belongs to you.

JOHN 10:27-29; GALATIANS 3:26, 29

What can I pray when I fear I'll be left out?
Don't let my heart be troubled. I trust in you, Jesus.
For you have said, "There is more than enough room
in my Father's home."   JOHN 14:1-2

Belonging to God's family means you are fully accepted by him.
Scripture assures you that you are worth the life of God's Son,
whom he sent to secure your salvation. Your place in the family of
God can never be taken away. When do you doubt that you're a
part of God's family? When you make mistakes? When you feel
detached from him? How might your own family history affect
the way you think about belonging to God's family?

BE OPEN TO CORRECTION

Lord, how do you convict me of sin?
All Scripture is inspired by me and is useful to teach you what is true and to make you realize what is wrong in your life. It corrects you when you are wrong and teaches you to do what is right. Let the Holy Spirit guide your life. The Spirit gives you desires that are the opposite of what your sinful nature desires.

2 TIMOTHY 3:16; GALATIANS 5:16-17

Do I need to be afraid of your discipline?
How can I be open to your correction?
Follow the Spirit's leading in every part of your life, for I am good and I do what is right. I show the proper path to those who go astray. I lead the humble in doing right, teaching them my way. I lead with unfailing love and faithfulness all who keep my covenant and obey my demands.

GALATIANS 5:25; PSALM 25:8-10

How can I pray for more openness to receive correction?
I won't reject your discipline, LORD, or be upset when you correct me. For you correct those you love, just as a father corrects a child in whom he delights.

PROVERBS 3:11-12

*W*hen the Holy Spirit convicts us, he points out where sin— instead of God's grace—is ruling our hearts. God sent his Spirit to you to encourage you in your faith and bring you back into right relationship with him. God's correction is always gentle and kind. If you are afraid that God will condemn you, or if you think your self-criticism is the voice of God, you will be closed off to his loving correction. What criticisms or self-condemnations might be preventing you from hearing the Holy Spirit calling you back to the Father?

CONFESSION ALWAYS ENDS WITH GOD'S MERCY

Lord, if confession strengthens my relationship with you, why is it so hard?

When the cool evening breezes were blowing, the man and his wife heard me walking about in the garden. So they hid from me among the trees. People who conceal their sins will not prosper, but if they confess and turn from them, they will receive mercy. The kind of sorrow I want you to experience leads you away from sin and results in salvation. There's no regret for that kind of sorrow.

GENESIS 3:8; PROVERBS 28:13;
2 CORINTHIANS 7:10

So how do I confess my sins to you?

Test and examine your ways. Turn back to me. Lift your heart and hands to me in heaven and say, "I have sinned and rebelled." If you confess your sins to me, I am faithful and just to forgive your sins and to cleanse you from all wickedness.

LAMENTATIONS 3:40-42; I JOHN 1:9

What prayer of confession can I offer to you, Lord?
I recognize my rebellion—it haunts me day and night.
Against you, and you alone, have I sinned; I have
done what is evil in your sight. Restore to me the joy
of your salvation, and make me willing to obey you.
You will not reject a broken and repentant heart.

PSALM 51:3-4, 12, 17

Guilt and shame always make us want to hide. Adam and Eve hid
in the garden and covered themselves with leaves after they sinned.
Their sin placed a relational barrier between themselves and God.
When sin separates you from God, confession is the bridge that
reconnects you. Where is guilt or shame causing you to hide from
God or others? The first step to restoration is bringing your sin
into the light so it can be washed away by God's forgiveness.

GROWING IN TRUST

Lord, what does it mean to trust you?
You love me even though you have never seen me.
Though you do not see me, you trust me; and you
rejoice with a glorious, inexpressible joy. Don't be
impressed with your own wisdom. Instead, fear me
and turn away from evil. Just as you accepted Christ
Jesus as your Lord, you must continue to follow him.
Let your roots grow down into him, and let your life
be built on him.

I PETER 1:8; PROVERBS 3:7; COLOSSIANS 2:6-7

What is the result of trusting you in this way?
Your faith will grow strong in the truth you were
taught, and you will overflow with thankfulness.
The reward for trusting me will be the salvation
of your soul.   COLOSSIANS 2:7; I PETER 1:9

What can I pray to trust you more?

Jesus, I pray that you will make your home in my heart as I trust in you; that my roots will grow down into your love and keep me strong.   EPHESIANS 3:17

Growing in your trust of God begins when you determine where it is difficult to trust him, and then choose to give in to his care. In what area of your life do you find it hard to trust God? Where do you have trouble letting go of control—life plans? Finances? How your kids turn out? Your marriage? What fears might be behind your need for control? Write your answers to these questions on a piece of paper, pray about them, and then throw away the paper as a symbol of releasing your control and choosing to grow your trust in God.

DO THE WORK. DON'T GIVE UP. GOD WILL HELP YOU.

Lord, how can I stay motivated to keep going when I feel discouraged?

Work willingly at whatever you do, as though you were working for me rather than for people. Those who live to please the Spirit will harvest everlasting life from the Spirit. Be strong and courageous, and do the work. Don't be afraid or discouraged, for I am with you. I will not fail you or forsake you. I help the fallen and lift those bent beneath their loads.

COLOSSIANS 3:23; GALATIANS 6:8;
I CHRONICLES 28:20; PSALM 145:14

What truth can I focus on when I'm tempted to believe my work doesn't matter?

Nothing you do for me is ever useless. So don't get tired of doing what is good. At just the right time you will reap a harvest of blessing if you don't give up.

I CORINTHIANS 15:58; GALATIANS 6:9

What can I pray when I need motivation to keep going?
For who is God except you, LORD? Who but my God
is a solid rock? You arm me with strength, and you
make my way perfect. You make me as surefooted as
a deer, enabling me to stand on mountain heights.

PSALM 18:31-33

Inspiration and enthusiasm can fade when you lose your sense of
purpose. But Scripture says that nothing you do for God is ever useless.
Sometimes what is needed is a clearer vision of your work and how
God can use it. If you're discouraged, ask God to give you fresh perspective and energy. Where do you need a renewed sense of motivation,
energy, and confidence? Write down this truth: "Nothing I do for
the Lord is ever useless." Allow it to help you move forward.

THE POWER OF GENTLENESS

Lord, why is gentleness important to you?
Since I chose you to be among the holy people I love,
you must clothe yourself with tenderhearted mercy,
kindness, humility, gentleness, and patience. Clothe
yourself with the beauty that comes from within, the
unfading beauty of a gentle and quiet spirit, which is
so precious to me. Take my yoke upon you. Let me
teach you, because I am humble and gentle at heart.

COLOSSIANS 3:12; I PETER 3:4; MATTHEW 11:29

How should I display gentleness as a follower of Jesus?
Pursue righteousness and a godly life, along with
faith, love, perseverance, and gentleness. A gentle
answer deflects anger, but harsh words make tem-
pers flare. Be kind to others, tenderhearted, for-
giving one another, just as I through Christ have
forgiven you.

I TIMOTHY 6:11; PROVERBS 15:1;
EPHESIANS 4:32

What can I pray when gentleness toward others feels hard?

Lord, make my love for others grow and overflow, just as your love for me overflows. Love is patient and kind. Love is not jealous or boastful or proud or rude. It does not demand its own way. It is not irritable, and it keeps no record of being wronged. Make my heart strong, blameless, and holy as I stand before you.

I THESSALONIANS 3:12; I CORINTHIANS 13:4-5; I THESSALONIANS 3:13

Gentleness is a characteristic of the Holy Spirit and a by-product of living a godly life. In God's eyes, gentle people have spiritual power because they make an impact through their kindness rather than through boasting or manipulation. The word gentle can be defined as "mild in temperament or behavior; kind or tender." Where in your life would you like to grow in one of these areas of gentleness? Consider the conversations and interactions you've had with others today, and pray the prayer above as you prepare for tomorrow.

EVERY DECISION IS AN OPPORTUNITY TO GAIN WISDOM

Lord, how can I avoid foolish choices?

Fools think their own way is right, but the wise listen to others. Those who trust their own insight are foolish, but anyone who walks in wisdom is safe. The prudent understand where they are going, but fools deceive themselves. A wise person is hungry for knowledge, while the fool feeds on trash.

PROVERBS 12:15; PROVERBS 28:26;
PROVERBS 14:8; PROVERBS 15:14

How do the consequences of foolishness compare with the benefits of seeking divine wisdom?

They hated knowledge and chose not to fear me. They rejected my advice and paid no attention when I corrected them. Therefore, they must eat the bitter fruit of living their own way, choking on their own schemes. For simpletons turn away from me—to death. Fools are destroyed by their own complacency. But all who listen to me will live in peace, untroubled by fear of harm.

PROVERBS 1:29-33

What can I pray to pursue your wise advice?
Keep me from lying to myself; give me the privilege of knowing your instructions. I have chosen to be faithful; I have determined to live by your regulations. I cling to your laws. LORD, don't let me be put to shame! I will pursue your commands, for you expand my understanding.   PSALM 119:29-32

Think about the decisions you need to make this week. These are all opportunities to seek God's wisdom. With each decision, ask yourself the following questions: Who can give me wise advice? What might happen to keep me from making or not making a particular choice? Is there truth from God's Word that can guide me? Have I prayed about it?

COMPASSION NEEDED

Lord, how do you show compassion?

I am like a father to my children, tender and compassionate to those who fear me. I care about you, and I will pay attention to you. I will rescue the poor when they cry to me; I will help the oppressed, who have no one to defend them. I feel pity for the weak and the needy, and I will rescue them. I will redeem them from oppression and violence, for their lives are precious to me.

PSALM 103:13; EZEKIEL 36:9; PSALM 72:12-14

How can I have compassion like this for others?

If someone has enough money to live well and sees a brother or sister in need but shows no compassion—how can my love be in that person? Learn to do good. Seek justice. When my people are in need, be ready to help them. Always be eager to practice hospitality. Don't be concerned for your own good but for the good of others. Share each other's burdens.

1 JOHN 3:17; ISAIAH 1:17; ROMANS 12:13;
1 CORINTHIANS 10:24; GALATIANS 6:2

*What can I pray out of gratitude for
your compassion to me?*

How kind you are! How good you are! So merciful,
O God of mine! You protect those of childlike faith;
I was facing death, and you saved me. Let my soul
be at rest again, for you have been good to me.

PSALM 116:5-7

*The world is full of people who desperately need to experience
the compassion that Jesus offers them. Because he is always loving,
tender, and full of sympathy toward us, how can we not act the same
way toward others? How has God shown compassion to you? Who
in your life needs to be shown that same compassion? Meet a need
of theirs this week. (For example: write an encouraging note, send
a thoughtful gift, forgive an offense, listen to their concerns.)*

CHOOSE JOY

Lord, how can I choose joy when I feel frustrated or disappointed with life?

Dear friends, don't be surprised at the fiery trials you are going through, as if something strange were happening to you. Instead, be very glad—for these trials make you partners with Christ in his suffering, so that you will have the wonderful joy of seeing his glory when it is revealed to all the world. Now you are deeply discouraged, but remember me. You hear the tumult of the raging seas as the waves and surging tides sweep over you. But each day I pour my unfailing love upon you, and through each night you sing my songs, praying to me who gives you life.

I PETER 4:12-13; PSALM 42:6-8

What example from your Word shows how to experience joy even in disappointment?

Then Nehemiah the governor, Ezra the priest and scribe, and the Levites who were interpreting for the people said to the people, "Don't mourn or weep on such a day as this! For today is a sacred day before the LORD your God." For the people had all been weeping as they listened to the words of the Law. And Nehemiah continued, "Go and celebrate with a feast of rich foods and sweet drinks, and share gifts of food with people who have nothing prepared. This is a sacred day before our Lord. Don't be dejected and sad, for the joy of the LORD is your strength!"

NEHEMIAH 8:9-10

What can I pray to rely on your joy as my strength?
Rise up, O LORD, in all your power. With music and singing I celebrate your mighty acts.   PSALM 21:13

God's presence with us and the work of Jesus Christ in us are always reasons for joy. Invite some friends or family over this week to celebrate and simply enjoy the blessings of life—friendship, good food, a great day, or even a small accomplishment. Choose to focus on joy and share your gratitude for God's unfailing love.

GROWING IN FAITH

Lord, how can my faith grow?

Faith shows the reality of what you hope for; it is the evidence of things you cannot see. By faith you understand that the entire universe was formed at my command, that what you now see did not come from anything that can be seen. Faith comes from hearing; that is, hearing the Good News about Christ. And I, who began the good work within you, will certainly continue my work until it is finally finished on the day when Christ Jesus returns.

HEBREWS 11:1, 3; ROMANS 10:17;
PHILIPPIANS 1:6

Am I the only one who struggles with doubt, Jesus?

I said to Thomas, "Put your finger here, and look at my hands. Put your hand into the wound in my side. Don't be faithless any longer. Believe!" "My Lord and my God!" Thomas exclaimed. Then I told him, "You believe because you have seen me. Blessed are those who believe without seeing me." JOHN 20:27-29

How can I pray for a stronger faith?

Fill me completely with joy and peace because I trust in you. Then I will overflow with confident hope through the power of the Holy Spirit.

ROMANS 15:13

Faith deepens our trust in God, even when we can't see him working. One of the ways our faith grows is when we hear stories of how God has worked and is working in the lives of others. This evening, read the entire chapter of Hebrews 11 for examples of people with great faith. Reflect on these questions: What encourages you to trust in God? What doubts or fears are keeping you from deeper trust in Jesus?

AS YOU GROW OLDER, CLING TO THIS

Lord, can you sympathize with the difficulty that comes from growing older?

I know how weak you are; I remember you are only dust. Your days on earth are like grass; like a wildflower, you bloom and die. While you live in this earthly body, you groan and sigh. You grow weary in your present body, and you long to put on your heavenly body like new clothing.

PSALM 103:14-15; 2 CORINTHIANS 5:4;
2 CORINTHIANS 5:2

What hope can I cling to as I struggle with aging?

My love remains forever with those who fear me. The godly will flourish. Even in old age they will still produce fruit; they will remain vital and green. Though your body is dying, your spirit is being renewed every day. I will take your weak mortal body and change it into a glorious body like my own.

PSALM 103:17; PROVERBS 14:11; PSALM 92:14;
2 CORINTHIANS 4:16; PHILIPPIANS 3:21

What can I pray when I need perspective on aging?

Father, you have been my guide since my youth. And now, in my old age, don't set me aside. Don't abandon me when my strength is failing. Teach me to realize the brevity of life, so that I may grow in wisdom. Satisfy me each morning with your unfailing love, so I may sing for joy to the end of my life.

JEREMIAH 3:4; PSALM 71:9; PSALM 90:12, 14

Talk to God about your fears of growing older. Are you tired of living with less energy? Discouraged about your body? Exhausted from health issues? How do today's Scriptures encourage you to trust God with your aging body and have hope for the eternal body he promises for those who trust him?

WHEN LIFE FEELS UNFAIR

Lord, do you really treat others fairly?

I am a shield, saving those whose hearts are true and right. I am an honest judge. I am angry with the wicked every day. Yet you say, "The Lord isn't doing what's right!" Listen to me. Am I the one not doing what's right, or is it you? My government and its peace will never end. I will rule with fairness and justice for all eternity.

PSALM 7:10-11; EZEKIEL 18:25; ISAIAH 9:7

How can I trust you when your ways don't seem fair?

My way is perfect. All my promises prove true. I am a shield for all who look to me for protection. I love justice, and I will never abandon the godly. I will keep them safe forever. I cause everything to work together for the good of those who love me and are called according to my purpose for them.

PSALM 18:30; PSALM 37:28; ROMANS 8:28

What can I pray to remind myself of your fairness?
In due season you will judge everyone, both good and bad, for all their deeds. I will thank you because you are just; I will sing praise to the name of the LORD Most High.

ECCLESIASTES 3:17; PSALM 7:17

A sense of fairness or unfairness means we are measuring our lives by some standard and judging whether it is in our favor. God is the only fair judge, and when we measure our life by his standard, we all fall short. We are all in desperate need of grace and a Savior. And his grace is most unfair because it is free and undeserved. What standard are you using to measure your life? What is something in your life that feels unfair? How might God's grace affect your perspective?

BE STRONG AND COURAGEOUS

Lord, where can I find courage to face my fears?
For who is God except me? Who besides me is a solid rock? I have not given you a spirit of fear and timidity, but of power, love, and self-discipline. So be strong and courageous! Do not be afraid and do not panic. I will personally go ahead of you. I will neither fail you nor abandon you.

PSALM 18:31; 2 TIMOTHY 1:7;
DEUTERONOMY 31:6

How can I be sure you will help me?
What is the price of two sparrows—one copper coin? But not a single sparrow can fall to the ground without my knowing it. And the very hairs on your head are all numbered. So don't be afraid; you are more valuable to me than a whole flock of sparrows.

MATTHEW 10:29-31

What can I pray when I need courage?

Hear me, LORD, and have mercy on me. Help me, O LORD. I entrust my spirit into your hand. Rescue me, LORD, for you are a faithful God. I will tell everyone about your power. Your strength is mighty in the heavens. You are awesome in your sanctuary. You give power and strength to your people. Praise be to you, God!

PSALM 30:10; PSALM 31:5; PSALM 68:34-35

Author Mark Twain once wrote, "Courage is resistance to fear, mastery of fear—not absence of fear."[5] There are times when you have no choice but to step into a situation that terrifies you. God can often use these moments to solidify your confidence in his presence and help. Even if you aren't feeling brave, you can face your fears with the assurance from God's Word that he is greater than any enemy or problem you are facing. Write out Hebrews 13:6: "The LORD is my helper, so I will have no fear. What can mere people do to me?" Memorize it to give you the courage to face your fears.

TIMES FOR WAITING

Lord, I believe you will keep your promises, but how can I patiently wait to see them fulfilled?
Patient endurance is what you need now, so that you will continue to do my will. Then you will receive all that I have promised. For you know that when your faith is tested, your endurance has a chance to grow. So let it grow, for when your endurance is fully developed, you will be perfect and complete, needing nothing. HEBREWS 10:36; JAMES 1:3-4

How can I use this time of waiting most wisely?
You will always harvest what you plant. Those who live only to satisfy their own sinful nature will harvest decay and death from that sinful nature. But those who live to please the Spirit will harvest everlasting life from the Spirit. So don't get tired of doing what is good. At just the right time you will reap a harvest of blessing if you don't give up. GALATIANS 6:7-9

How can I pray while I wait?

I am confident I will see your goodness, LORD, while I am here in the land of the living. I will wait patiently for you, LORD. I will be brave and courageous. Yes, I will wait patiently for you, LORD. The Scriptures give me hope and encouragement as I wait patiently for your promises to be fulfilled.

PSALM 27:13-14; ROMANS 15:4

What are you planting in this season of your life? What is the harvest you are patiently waiting for right now? Perhaps it's renewed love with your spouse or obedience in your child. How can you use this time of waiting to please the Lord and do good? Here are some examples: You can plant seeds of forgiveness in your marriage; give grace and a gentle response to a rebellious child; choose vegetables over sweets to plant seeds of health; give generously to show you are trusting in God's provision.

GOD'S RESCUE PLAN

*Lord, are you doing anything about all the
pain in the world?*

I have seen violence done to the helpless, and I have
heard the groans of the poor. Now I will rise up to rescue them, as they have longed for me to do. I will rescue those who love me. I will protect those who trust
in my name. When they call on me, I will answer;
I will be with them in trouble. I will rescue them and
honor them.

PSALM 12:5; PSALM 91:14-15

What is your rescue plan?

There is one Mediator who can reconcile humanity
with me—the man Christ Jesus. He gave his life to
purchase freedom for everyone. This is the message I
gave to the world at just the right time. Jesus gave his
life for your sins, just as I planned, in order to rescue
you from this evil world in which you live.

I TIMOTHY 2:5-6; GALATIANS 1:4

*What can I pray in response to the pain
I see in the world?*

I put my hope in you, LORD. You are my help and my
shield. Arise, O LORD! Punish the wicked, O God! Do
not ignore the helpless! LORD, you know the hopes of
the helpless. Surely you will hear their cries and comfort them. You will bring justice.

PSALM 33:20; PSALM 10:12, 17-18

*God isn't ignoring pain and suffering in the world today. He is
acting to rescue people, even if we can't see it. Separation from God
because of sin is ultimately why this world so badly needs a Savior.
Jesus gave his life to make a way for the world to be reconciled to
God. Memorize Psalm 33:20: "We put our hope in the LORD. He is
our help and our shield." Claim these words as a promise of hope
today. When you encounter pain or hear of violence or evil in
the world, use this verse to declare your hope in God's rescue.*

MONEY DOESN'T BUY HAPPINESS

*Lord, what principles can guide me in
being wise with my finances?*

Those who love money will never have enough. How
meaningless to think that wealth brings true happiness!
Wealth from get-rich-quick schemes quickly disappears;
wealth from hard work grows over time. Honor me with
your wealth and with the best part of everything you
produce. Then I will fill your barns with grain, and your
vats will overflow with good wine.

ECCLESIASTES 5:10; PROVERBS 13:11;
PROVERBS 3:9-10

*How can I fight against always wanting
just a little more?*

True godliness with contentment is itself great wealth.
After all, you brought nothing with you when you
came into the world, and you can't take anything with
you when you leave it. So if you have enough food
and clothing, be content.   1 TIMOTHY 6:6-8

What can I pray to get my heart in the right place when making financial decisions?

Father, help me not to love money, and to be satisfied with what I have. For you have said, "I will never fail you. I will never abandon you."   HEBREWS 13:5

Walk through your home and take an inventory of your possessions. Thank and praise God for every good thing. Ask him to fill you with contentment for what you have been given. How do you feel after this activity? Do you find yourself more content? Are you more thankful?

INVITE THE LORD INTO EVERY AREA OF YOUR LIFE

Lord, do I need to invite you into my day, or are you already here?

I am with you always. I am living among you. I am a mighty savior. I take delight in you with gladness. With my love, I will calm all your fears. I rejoice over you with joyful songs. For I hold you by your right hand—I, the LORD your God. Don't be afraid. I am here to help you. If you look for me wholeheartedly, you will find me.

MATTHEW 28:20; ZEPHANIAH 3:17; ISAIAH 41:13; JEREMIAH 29:13

How can I also remember to invite you into my plans, thoughts, and interactions with others?

Devote yourselves to prayer with an alert mind and a thankful heart. Seek me while you can find me. Call on me now while I am near. My love remains forever with those who fear me. My child, never forget the things I have taught you. Store my commands in your heart.

COLOSSIANS 4:2; ISAIAH 55:6; PSALM 103:17; PROVERBS 3:1

*What can I pray to remind myself that
you are always near?*

You are near, O LORD, and all your commands are
true. I have known from my earliest days that your
laws will last forever. LORD, you are good, a strong
refuge when trouble comes. You are close to those
who trust in you.

PSALM 119:151-152; NAHUM 1:7

When you invite God into your day, it isn't to convince him to be
present. He has already promised to be with you in every moment.
You invite God into your day to increase your awareness of his presence. Remembering God's presence gives you peace and helps you
enter situations with him at the forefront of your mind. If you are
facing a challenging conversation, meeting, or situation, take a
deep breath and prayerfully invite God to be with you in it—
remembering that he has already promised to be there.

THIS IS SACRIFICIAL LOVE

*Lord, why did you need to sacrifice
your Son on the cross?*

I did what the law could not do. I sent my own
Son in a body like the bodies you sinners have.
And in that body I declared an end to sin's control
over you. This is real love—not that you loved me,
but that I loved you and sent my Son as a sacrifice
to take away your sins. He personally carried your
sins in his own body on the cross so that you can
be dead to sin and live for what is right. By his
wounds you are healed.

ROMANS 8:3; I JOHN 4:10; I PETER 2:24

What kinds of sacrifices do you ask me to make?

Give your bodies to me because of all I have done for
you. Let them be a living and holy sacrifice. Live a
life filled with love, following the example of Christ,
who loved you and offered himself as a sacrifice
for you.   ROMANS 12:1; EPHESIANS 5:2

How can I pray for a sacrificial heart?

Show me where to walk, for I give myself to you.
Above all, may I live as a citizen of heaven, conduct-
ing myself in a manner worthy of the Good News
about Christ. I will rejoice even if I lose my life,
pouring it out like a liquid offering to you.

PSALM 143:8; PHILIPPIANS 1:27;
PHILIPPIANS 2:17

Sacrifice is not just giving things up; rather, it is a substitution. You give up one thing to obtain something of greater value. God uses your sacrifices to shape your heart to be more like his—one that is more loving, selfless, and generous. Read Philippians 2:5-7: "Have the same attitude that Christ Jesus had. Though he was God, he did not think of equality with God as something to cling to. Instead, he gave up his divine privileges; he took the humble position of a slave." What words from this passage stand out to you and most touch your heart? Meditate on what God has sacrificed for you.

YOUR SALVATION IS SECURE

Lord, how can I be sure my salvation is secure?
This is how I loved the world: I gave my one and only Son, so that everyone who believes in him will not perish but have eternal life. Everyone who calls on my name will be saved. I give them eternal life, and they will never perish. No one can snatch them away from me, for I am more powerful than anyone else.

JOHN 3:16; ROMANS 10:13; JOHN 10:28-29

What can remind me of your power to secure my salvation?
Very early on Sunday morning the women went to the tomb. They found that the stone had been rolled away from the entrance. So they went in, but they didn't find the body of the Lord Jesus. Two men suddenly appeared to them, clothed in dazzling robes. The women were terrified and bowed with their faces to the ground. Then the men asked, "Why are you

looking among the dead for someone who is alive? He isn't here! He is risen from the dead!" LUKE 24:1-6

What can I pray when I feel insecure about my salvation?

LORD, you are my light and my salvation—so why should I be afraid? You are my fortress, protecting me from danger, so why should I tremble? Though a mighty army surrounds me, my heart will not be afraid. Even if I am attacked, I will remain confident. PSALM 27:1, 3

Whenever you doubt God's promise of salvation to those who believe in him, recite the psalm above as a prayer. Read this psalm before bed every night this week, asking God to help your heart fully trust these words.

HOW TO MANAGE
THE OVERWHELMING

Lord, how can I cope when life is overwhelming?
Trust in me at all times. Pour out your heart to me,
for I am your refuge. Give your burdens to me, and I
will take care of you. Never give up, for your present
troubles are small and won't last very long. Yet they
produce for you a glory that vastly outweighs them
and will last forever! You who have fled to me for refuge can have great confidence as you hold to the hope
that lies before you. This hope is a strong and trust-
worthy anchor for your soul.

PSALM 62:8; PSALM 55:22;
2 CORINTHIANS 4:16-17; HEBREWS 6:18-19

What is my greatest hope?
My home will be among my people! I myself will be
with them. I will wipe every tear from their eyes, and
there will be no more death or sorrow or crying or
pain. All these things will be gone forever.

REVELATION 21:3-4

What can I pray when I don't know how to cope?
Please listen and answer me, for I am overwhelmed by
my troubles. I am worn out from sobbing. All night
I flood my bed with weeping, drenching it with my
tears. But I called on your name, LORD, from deep
within the pit. You heard me when I cried, "Listen to
my pleading! Hear my cry for help!" Yes, you came
when I called; you told me, "Do not fear."

PSALM 55:2; PSALM 6:6; LAMENTATIONS 3:55-57

There are many effective ways to cope with pain, but one way
you must not neglect is clinging to the Lord, who provides your
ultimate hope and healing. Take a moment to pour out your heart
to God. Then sit in silence for a minute and breathe in deeply,
remembering that he is with you, caring for you in your pain.

GOD IS LOVE

Lord, how is your love different from human love?
I am love, and all who live in love live in me, and I
live in them. My faithful love endures forever. My
faithful love never ends! My mercies never cease.
I always fulfill my covenant and keep my promises
of unfailing love to those who love me and obey
my commands.

1 JOHN 4:16; PSALM 136:1; LAMENTATIONS 3:22;
DANIEL 9:4

How powerful is your love?
Can anything ever separate you from my love? Does
it mean I no longer love you if you have trouble or
calamity, or are persecuted, or hungry, or destitute,
or in danger, or threatened with death? Nothing can
ever separate you from my love. Neither death nor
life, neither angels nor demons, neither your fears for
today nor your worries about tomorrow—not even
the powers of hell can separate you from my love.

ROMANS 8:35, 38

What can I pray to experience the fullness of your love?
May I have the power to understand, as all your
people should, how wide, how long, how high, and
how deep your love is. May I experience the love of
Christ, though it is too great to understand fully.
Then I will be made complete with all the fullness
of life and power that comes from you.

EPHESIANS 3:18-19

In your human relationships, you may love deeply but never perfectly. Your love may last a lifetime, but it will never have the unshakable faithfulness and eternal power of God's love for you. Every heartache, betrayal, or hurt is meant to point you to your need for God's faithful, perfect, eternal love. Close your eyes and imagine God looking at you with total approval and love. What does this feel like? Thank him right now that nothing can separate you from his love.

GOD'S VOICE ALWAYS ENCOURAGES AND NEVER CONDEMNS

Lord, how can I know the difference between Satan's accusations and your convictions?

Stay alert! Watch out for your great enemy, the devil. He prowls around like a roaring lion, looking for someone to devour. The thief's purpose is to steal and kill and destroy. My purpose is to give you a rich and satisfying life. I am the good shepherd. The good shepherd sacrifices his life for the sheep.

1 PETER 5:8; JOHN 10:10-11

But how can I be strong enough to fight against Satan?

Pray in the Spirit at all times and on every occasion. Stay alert and be persistent in your prayers. As soon as you pray, I answer you. I encourage you by giving you strength. Be strong in me and in my mighty power. For you are not fighting against flesh-and-blood enemies, but against evil rulers and authorities of the unseen world, against mighty powers in this dark world, and against evil spirits in the heavenly places. But I am faithful; I will strengthen you and guard you from the evil one.

EPHESIANS 6:18; PSALM 138:3;
EPHESIANS 6:10, 12; 2 THESSALONIANS 3:3

*What can I pray when I feel accused
and attacked by Satan?*

O LORD, oppose those who oppose me. Fight those who fight against me. Put on your armor, and take up your shield. Prepare for battle, and come to my aid. Let me hear you say, "I will give you victory!" Then I will rejoice in you. I will be glad because you rescue me.

PSALM 35:1-3, 9

It is important to know how to discern between Satan's lies and God's truth. Lies from Satan might sound true, but they will come with accusations, discouragement, and condemnation. God's truth may hurt, but it always comes with grace, gentleness, love, and mercy. Where do you feel accused? Pray that God would replace any lies with his truth.

ARE YOU PREPARED TO EXPLAIN YOUR HOPE?

Lord, how can I begin to look for opportunities to tell others about you?

The harvest is great, but the workers are few. So pray to the Lord who is in charge of the harvest; ask him to send more workers into his fields. And if someone asks about your hope as a believer, always be ready to explain it. Let your conversation be gracious and attractive so that you will have the right response for everyone.

MATTHEW 9:37-38; I PETER 3:15;
COLOSSIANS 4:6

How can I know when you're providing me an opportunity to share about who you are?

Philip met the treasurer of Ethiopia, who had gone to Jerusalem to worship. Philip ran over and heard the man reading from the prophet Isaiah. Philip asked, "Do you understand what you are reading?" The man replied, "How can I, unless someone instructs me?" So beginning with this same Scripture, Philip told him the Good News about me. Come, follow me, and I will show you how to fish for people!

ACTS 8:27, 30-31, 35; MATTHEW 4:19

What can I pray to make the most of my opportunities to share my faith?
LORD, have you redeemed me? Then I must speak out! Help me tell others that you have redeemed me from my enemies. How can others hear about you unless someone tells them? Here I am. Send me.

PSALM 107:2; ROMANS 10:14; ISAIAH 6:8

If someone asked you why you follow Jesus, what would you say? Write your response down. If you don't have a ready response, spend some time reflecting on where you've seen the Lord at work in your life. What reasons do you have to be confident in God's love for you? What have you been thankful for? Sharing your personal experience can be the most powerful witness. Pray for God to provide an opportunity for you to share the Good News with someone.

CREATION IS ALWAYS SPEAKING ABOUT THE CREATOR

Lord, how do you reveal yourself through your creation?

Ever since the world was created, people have seen the earth and sky. Through everything I made, they can clearly see my invisible qualities—my eternal power and divine nature. The heavens proclaim my glory. The skies display my craftsmanship. Day after day they continue to speak; night after night they make me known. I am the great King of all the earth.

ROMANS 1:20; PSALM 19:1-2; PSALM 47:2

What can I learn about you from your creation?

Look at the birds. They don't plant or harvest or store food in barns, for I feed them. And aren't you far more valuable to me than they are? Can all your worries add a single moment to your life? MATTHEW 6:26-27

*What can I pray when I'm overwhelmed by
the beauty of your creation?*

O LORD my God, how great you are! You stretch out
the starry curtain of the heavens; you lay out the raf-
ters of your home in the rain clouds. Such knowledge
is too wonderful for me, too great for me to understand! O Sovereign LORD! You made the heavens and
earth by your strong hand and powerful arm. Nothing
is too hard for you!

PSALM 104:1-3; PSALM 139:6; JEREMIAH 32:17

Creation is just one of the many ways that God reveals himself to us.
The vastness and beauty of God's world reminds us of his power, and
the fine details remind us of his wisdom. Go outside this evening—
even if just for a minute. Look around and find something that
moves you to worship your creator. Let God's world remind you of
his great love and awesome power over what he has created.

EMBRACE WHO GOD MADE YOU TO BE

Lord, how can I embrace the unique way in which you made me?
I made all the delicate, inner parts of your body and knit you together in your mother's womb. I made you wonderfully complex! My workmanship is marvelous. I saw you before you were born. Every day of your life was recorded in my book. Every moment was laid out before a single day had passed.

PSALM 139:13-14, 16

My life is by your design, but why? For what purpose?
I knew you and chose you long ago, and my Spirit has made you holy. In my grace, I have given you different gifts for doing certain things well. Just as your body has many parts and each part has a special function, so it is with Christ's body. I have put each part just where I want it.

I PETER 1:2; ROMANS 12:6; ROMANS 12:4-5; I CORINTHIANS 12:18

What can I pray to feel more secure in my uniqueness?
God, you formed me, and you say, "Do not be afraid,
for I have ransomed you. I have called you by name;
you are mine." ISAIAH 43:1

C. S. Lewis writes, "If all experienced God in the same way and returned Him an identical worship, the song of the Church triumphant would have no symphony, it would be like an orchestra in which all the instruments played the same note."[6] God made you one of a kind because he needs you to play your part in the symphony of his church. Listen to Beethoven's Third Symphony. Try to pick out individual notes. While you listen, prayerfully ask the Holy Spirit to reveal where you're trying to play someone else's note and how you can embrace the note that God has given you to play.

DON'T GIVE UP ON WHAT YOU'VE BEEN CALLED TO DO

Lord, how can I pursue my calling when I feel so inadequate?

Don't get tired of doing what is good. At just the right time you will reap a harvest of blessing if you don't give up. Be strong and courageous, and do the work. Don't be afraid or discouraged, for I am with you. I will not fail you or forsake you.

GALATIANS 6:9; I CHRONICLES 28:20

How do you reward those who faithfully serve you to the end?

You will receive the crown of life that I have promised to those who love me. I will say, "Well done, my good and faithful servant. You have been faithful in handling this small amount, so now I will give you many more responsibilities. Let's celebrate together!"

JAMES 1:12; MATTHEW 25:23

What can I pray when I need encouragement to press on?
I am pressed on every side by troubles, but I am not crushed. I am perplexed, but not driven to despair. I know that you, God, who raised the Lord Jesus, will also raise me with Jesus and present me to yourself. That is why I never give up.

2 CORINTHIANS 4:8, 14, 16

If God has called you to a task, don't give up when it gets difficult. Just because God asks you to do something doesn't mean it will be easy. Sometimes the things that are most worth doing are the hardest. Don't worry about whether you are adequate for the task. Your job is simply to wake up each morning and ask God to help you faithfully obey him. Write down Philippians 4:13: "I can do everything through Christ, who gives me strength." Put it where it's easily visible. Remind yourself that with God's help, you are able to accomplish everything he calls you to do.

YOU CAN POINT THE WAY

Lord, how can I point children to Jesus?
You must love me with all your heart, all your soul,
and all your strength. And you must commit yourself wholeheartedly to these commands that I am
giving you today. Repeat them again and again to
your children. Talk about them when you are at
home and when you are on the road, when you are
going to bed and when you are getting up.

DEUTERONOMY 6:5-7

What is the impact of this kind of example?
Do not hide these truths from your children; tell the
next generation about my glorious deeds, about my
power and my mighty wonders. I commanded your
ancestors to teach my instructions to their children,
so the next generation might know them—even the
children not yet born—and they in turn will teach
their own children. So each generation should set its
hope anew on me, not forgetting my glorious miracles and obeying my commands. Then they will

learn that I alone am called the LORD, that I alone am the Most High, supreme over all the earth.

PSALM 78:4-7; PSALM 83:18

What can I pray when I feel insufficient as a parent?
So if we sinful people know how to give good gifts to our children, how much more will you, our heavenly Father, give good gifts to those who ask you?

MATTHEW 7:11

Teaching children God's ways and pointing them to the grace of Jesus is one of the greatest gifts you can offer. It will have an impact on generations to come. Pray right now for your children, your grandchildren, and your great-grandchildren to continue the legacy of faith. Look for an opportunity to share Jesus with your children this evening. Read them a Bible story before bed, pray about what's bothering them, or share what God is doing in your life. If you don't have children, pray for a child you know.

THE SABBATH WAS CREATED FOR YOU

Lord, do you still want me to keep the Sabbath?
The Sabbath was made to meet the needs of people, and not people to meet the requirements of the Sabbath. You have six days each week for your ordinary work, but the seventh day is a Sabbath day of rest dedicated to me. The Sabbath is a sign of the covenant between me and you from generation to generation. It is given so you may know that I am the LORD, who makes you holy.

MARK 2:27; EXODUS 20:9-10; EXODUS 31:13

How can I rest for a whole day without feeling guilty?
On the seventh day I had finished my work of creation, so I rested from all my work. And I blessed the seventh day and declared it holy, because it was the day when I rested from all my work. Keep the Sabbath day holy. Don't pursue your own interests on that day, but enjoy the Sabbath and speak of it with delight as my holy day.   GENESIS 2:2-3; ISAIAH 58:13

What can I pray before I enter into Sabbath rest?

You, LORD, are my shepherd; I have all that I need.
You let me rest in green meadows; you lead me beside
peaceful streams. You renew my strength. There is a
special rest still waiting for your people. For all who
enter into your rest will find rest from their labors,
just as you rested after creating the world.

PSALM 23:1-3; HEBREWS 4:9-10

Both God's Word and Jesus' example make it clear that setting
aside time for rest and refreshment is essential for restoring both
body and soul. Sabbath gives us permission to let go of our to-do
lists for twenty-four hours and trust God with the things left
undone. Think about the people, places, and activities that help
you rest and draw your attention back to God. What can you let
go of to make space for these things during the next Sabbath?

EVEN PERFECTION
HAS ITS LIMITS

Lord Jesus, I feel so much pressure to have the perfect house, kids, vacations, etc. What does your Word say about striving for perfection?

Mary sat at my feet, listening to what I taught. But Martha was distracted by the big dinner she was preparing. She came to me and said, "Lord, doesn't it seem unfair to you that my sister just sits here while I do all the work? Tell her to come and help me." But I said to her, "My dear Martha, you are worried and upset over all these details! There is only one thing worth being concerned about. Mary has discovered it, and it will not be taken away from her."

LUKE 10:39-42

How can I stop striving for perfection and rest in your perfect work?

After starting your new lives in the Spirit, why are you now trying to become perfect by your own human effort? For by the power of the eternal Spirit,

Christ offered himself to me as a perfect sacrifice
for your sins.

GALATIANS 3:3; HEBREWS 9:14

What can I pray to remember that only you are perfect?
God, your way is perfect. Even perfection has its lim-
its, but your commands have no limit.

PSALM 18:30; PSALM 119:96

*Every day, we are bombarded by images of perfection. Magazines,
TV shows, websites—the message they all send is that perfection
is attainable! Do something this week that you know you won't do
perfectly. Play an instrument you haven't practiced recently, draw
a picture, cook a complicated recipe. Try to embrace this
motto: It doesn't have to be perfect to be good. Ask the Lord to
help you embrace goodness without the illusion of perfection.*

BE FAITHFUL IN THE LITTLE THINGS

Lord, what does a life of integrity look like?
Joyful are people of integrity, who follow my instructions. Joyful are those who obey my laws and search for me with all their hearts; those who do what is right, speaking the truth from sincere hearts; those who refuse to gossip or harm their neighbors or speak evil of their friends; those who keep their promises even when it hurts.   PSALM 119:1-2; PSALM 15:2-4

How can I develop greater integrity?
If you are faithful in little things, you will be faithful in large ones. But if you are dishonest in little things, you won't be honest with greater responsibilities. Choose today whom you will serve.

LUKE 16:10; JOSHUA 24:15

*How can I pray for integrity in
a morally tricky situation?*

I know, my God, that you examine my heart and
rejoice when you find integrity there. Oh, that my
actions would consistently reflect your decrees!

I CHRONICLES 29:17; PSALM 119:5

*Integrity is the alignment of your character with God's charac-
ter. It reflects the heart, mind, and actions of God as much as is
humanly possible. But integrity isn't something you achieve
instantly; developing it is a process that happens choice by choice.
If you can be trusted to be honest in a small matter, you will
eventually be trusted to be honest in larger matters. Is there a
small decision where you feel tempted to cut a corner, tell a white
lie, or act apart from God's character? Ask yourself if you'd
trust someone else who didn't act with integrity. Are you willing
to act with integrity no matter what the outcome?*

WHAT DO YOU WANT GOD TO DO FOR YOU?

*Lord, are you sensitive toward the hardships
and hurts in my life?*
I am merciful and compassionate, slow to get angry
and filled with unfailing love. I am good to everyone.
I shower compassion on all my creation. I hear my
people when they call to me for help. I rescue them
from all their troubles.

PSALM 145:8-9; PSALM 34:17

How can I catch a glimpse of your sensitivity, Jesus?
Two blind men were sitting beside the road. When
they heard that I was coming that way, they began
shouting, "Lord, Son of David, have mercy on us!"
When I heard them, I stopped and called, "What do
you want me to do for you?" "Lord," they said, "we
want to see!" I felt sorry for them and touched their
eyes. Instantly they could see!

MATTHEW 20:30, 32-34

What can I pray to remind myself of your sensitivity toward my pain?

I love you, LORD, because you hear my voice and my prayer for mercy. Because you bend down to listen, I will pray as long as I have breath! How kind you are! How good you are! So merciful, this God of mine!

PSALM 116:1-2, 5

God does not feel annoyed or frustrated during your seasons of hardship. In fact, he promises to respond with sensitivity to your pain. He listens to your prayers, shows you mercy and kindness, and helps you in your troubles. Just as Jesus had mercy toward the blind men crying out to him in their pain, he longs to be merciful toward you in yours. Talk to God about something hard or painful in your life. Imagine him sitting with you, listening intently to your prayer. What sensitive words of compassion might he be speaking to you tonight?

NOTES

1. See Hebrews 4.
2. Psalm 92:2.
3. Adapted from Psalm 116:7.
4. C. S. Lewis, *The Lion, the Witch and the Wardrobe* (New York: HarperCollins, 2008), 80.
5. Mark Twain, *Pudd'nhead Wilson* (Mineola, NY: Dover Publications, 1999), 60.
6. C. S. Lewis, *The Problem of Pain* (New York: HarperCollins, 2001), 156.